WIN at HOME FIRST

AN INSPIRATIONAL GUIDE TO WORK-LIFE BALANCE

CORY M. CARLSON

Win at Home First: An Inspirational Guide to Work-Life Balance
Published by Cloud Rider Publishing
Cincinnati, OH

Some names and identifying details have been changed to protect the privacy of those involved.

Unless otherwise indicated, all Scripture quotations are taken from the Holy Bible, English Standard Version, copyright 2001 by Crossway Bibles, Good News Publishers.

Library of Congress Control Number: 2019901470
ISBN: 978-1-7337671-0-1
BUSINESS & ECONOMICS / Personal Success

QUANTITY PURCHASES: Companies, professional groups, clubs, and other organizations may qualify for special terms when ordering quantities of this title. For information, email cory@corymcarlson.com.

CLOUD RIDER
PUBLISHING

PRAISE FOR *WIN AT HOME FIRST*

"*Win at Home First* is spot on. The combination of testimony and tools make this book transformational for the individual who wants to be a positive leader."

Jon Gordon, bestselling author of
*The Power of Positive Leadership and The Carpente*r

"I'm thankful for *Win at Home First*. The pathway to truly winning in life is exactly opposite of the way we've all been taught, and I'm thankful for the reminder. Just like you, I want to win. Cory is pointing the way."

Brian Tome, founder and senior pastor of Crossroads
Church and author of *The Five Marks of a Man*

"In his book, *Win at Home First*, Cory M. Carlson produces a thought-provoking, logical progression of priorities that sets the stage for operational success in all dimensions of life."

Chad Williams, former Navy SEAL and
bestselling author of *SEAL of God*

"If you are trying to do it all at both work and home and find yourself stressed out, this is the book for you. Cory's stories are real, raw and will connect with what you feel but have never said out loud. *Win at Home First* will help you keep your family close, prioritize at work, and move you closer to the coveted but elusive work-life balance in a way you can win at both."

Jody Maberry, Host of *Creating Disney Magic*

"Authentic. Practical. Encouraging and enlightening. *Win at Home First* brought clarity of thought and vision to a struggle I seem to encounter often: life balance. Often we calibrate our life to work versus home and yet home is the key to success at work. This is a great book that calibrates the right work-life balance for success in both areas of life. A must read."

Chris Hartenstein, CEO of Hartco, Inc., and
founder of The New Frontier

DEDICATION

This book is dedicated to my wife, Holly.
Your grace, mercy, unconditional love, and forgiveness
is why I was able to write this book. Thanks for being
by my side this entire journey.

ILU—Cory

TABLE OF CONTENTS

Part 2—MARRIAGE

Part 3—PARENTING

Part 4—WORK

FOREWORD

We all want to win.

We want the joy of setting a goal and hitting it. We want the accolades of progress, the praise of those around us, and the rush of new opportunities and potential deals coming our way. We want to win—the question is "How?" Culture doesn't help here—to look around at the headlines and our news feeds, it seems like success is everywhere. We all think we know winning when we see it. It's the high-powered exec flying from meeting to speaking engagement to new business acquisition. It's the athlete or entertainer launching a new product line. It's that family down the street with a revolving door of new cars and flashy toys. We stand by and watch, assuming that they've got some advantage we don't—smarter, more money, more connections, or just plain lucky. Regardless, they seem to have won, and they're reaping the benefits. Yet all too often, those "success" stories crash and burn. Those people we envied end up having as much chaos and stress as we do.

We need a different path, because sacrificing everything we've got at the altar of corporate titles, personal brands, and body beautiful simply isn't working.

This is why I'm thankful for Cory.

First, I'm thankful for his story. I'm thankful that he's a guy who has done the hard work of following God through uncertainty, risk, and fear. I'm thankful that he's been willing to walk through (and be honest about) the costs of honesty. I'm thankful that he's seen the freedom and clarity that comes when you let God reorient your priorities and resources. And I'm thankful for his courage in living a completely countercultural journey.

Cory has been a part of the church I lead for the last eight years. He has been faithful in numerous roles with us. He has a gentle, uplifting demeanor that elevates the game of those around him. He has put his time and energy where his mouth and pen are. He is a man who practices what he preaches in this book.

Second, I'm thankful for his work. He has distilled years of personal experience and the collective wisdom and frameworks of some of the most impactful spiritual and professional organizations in the world. What you hold in your hands are battle-tested principles that have been proven time and time again. We live in a world that is constantly telling us to self-promote, to accumulate, to climb the ladder. Our culture says that if you want to win, get out there and make a name for yourself. In the face of that message, Cory challenges us to look in a different direction—to put God at the center. To focus on your personal life and your home long before you think about work. To think less about success and more about significance.

Put simply, I'm thankful for the message Cory is proclaiming—both with his writing and his life. The pathway to truly winning in life is exactly opposite of the way we've all been taught, and I'm thankful for the reminder.

Just like you, I want to win. Cory is pointing the way.

Brian Tome
Founder and senior pastor of Crossroads Church
and author of *The Five Marks of a Man*

INTRODUCTION

A little over ten years ago, I was sitting in a church classroom with eight other people in Denver, Colorado. Our group had just started a class taught by our pastor, Jay Pathak, called "Equip." We were studying to be future volunteer leaders, learning core values and principles so that we would speak the same vocabulary and have some common tools.

This particular Thursday night the discussion was about character. Jay talked about the importance of character not only for staff members but also for key volunteer leaders so that we could lead from a better position as well as never be a distraction to the movement and progress of the church. I loved hearing Jay speak—his humor and intelligence—so I was excited for this teaching series and to spend more time with Jay.

As Jay was talking about character that night, the weirdest feeling came over me. I could not really make out the words Jay was saying anymore. The whole class was a blur. As I looked around the room, I could see the other people, but I just felt like I was mentally in a different place. It was this abstract feeling, kind of floating, kind of numb, although I knew I was still in the chair.

Right then it hit me. "You have to come clean about your affair." What??? What was that voice? Who said that? Again, I heard, "You have to come clean about your affair." In the past I had often felt guilty about having had an affair, but I just shook the feeling off. I would go for a run, or have a drink, or do something else to distract me from my conscience.

This time was different. I knew it was God.

For the next few minutes I had this mental wrestling match with God.

"Why?!" I said. "No way!" I don't know what this internal conversation looked like to the other people in the room. I had to look dazed and confused.

I started to build my case to God for why I was not going to come clean about my affair.

"The affair happened years ago. In a different city. I stopped talking to the other woman when we ended the affair. I am not even connected with her on social media. She is married and has kids, so she will never say anything about the affair. We never had sex. I am a different person now than I was then. I now have two daughters, and I can't lose my marriage and my connection to my daughters. Plus, work is going great. I just got promoted and we moved to Denver. I'm managing a team, making more money than ever. Life is good. If I tell Holly, it could totally backfire. It would be stupid. She could leave me. Others would find out I had an affair. People would think I'm a fraud. Can't we just keep this between us, God?"

A GREATER STORY

Then I heard God reply, "You have to hand over your small story for a greater story." *What? What does that mean?* My guard was back up.

"If I tell my story, that could be the end. Divorce. See my daughters only on weekends. Holly and my daughters would move back to Missouri close to her parents, and I'd be stuck in Denver by myself. I probably would need to move back to Missouri."

I started to feel like a failure. *What happened to me? I grew up in an amazing home with an amazing mom and dad who modeled a great marriage. How did I screw up this bad? What are people going to think of me?*

Again, I heard God say (not audibly, but still clearly), "You have to hand over your small story for a greater story."

Finally, my mind started to shift from defensive to curious. What is this greater story? What does it mean?

A peace started to come upon me. A warmth. I felt I was being invited into an adventure. Not condemnation, but an invitation. I began to feel I needed to tell Holly about my affair. I didn't need to run from this anymore. I had no idea what her reaction would be or what the fallout would be, but I had a peace that I would get through it. I even had a hope that we, together, would get through it. I began to feel a freedom of breaking these chains that had held me back for so many years. I could feel the veil that covered my true self start to lift.

As I left that night, I was determined to tell Holly. On the drive home I prayed. Prayed for help, for direction, for guidance about where this was going to take me. I also said prayers of, "God, are you sure? Let's just keep this between us. Me and you. Nobody else has to know." But God wasn't having it.

When I got home, Holly was asleep. *Woohoo!* I thought. I didn't have to tell her. It wasn't meant to be! If God really wanted me to come clean, she would be awake and waiting for me. I went to bed.

The next morning, I woke up and had the feeling I needed to tell her, but I ignored it. Just like I had for the last five years. The rest of the day we ran errands. That night we actually had a friend's party to go to. As the day went on, though, the feeling from the night before started coming back to me. The invitation to adventure. Handing over my story for a greater story. Maybe my story was going to be used to help others. As the day progressed, I was building up the courage to tell her.

When we got home that night, after I put our daughters to bed, I went downstairs to the laundry room where Holly was folding clothes. I took a deep breath, and I told her I had an affair years earlier when we lived in Kansas City. I told her who the woman was. Told her I hadn't talked to her in years. Told her how it started. Answered the questions she had.

She later told me that as I was talking, the Holy Spirit came over her and said, "It will be OK." Now that doesn't mean it was cupcakes and balloons at the Carlson household. It was exactly what you would expect. Yelling, doors slamming, tears, more yelling, more tears. It sucked, and rightfully so.

I was an idiot, and I had made a selfish and dumb mistake. I broke our vows. I broke her trust. I betrayed her. I had been living a lie for years.

Thankfully, Holly hung onto the phrase "It will be OK" for the next few months as we tried to work through it. I am sure she reminds herself of those exact words still to this day when I am being difficult to live with!

Through her unbelievable grace, mercy, and forgiveness, we got through it. The road to our marriage restoration began to take shape as well as our own personal journeys and restoration.

This book contains some of the key tools and concepts God used to restore Holly and me individually and as a couple, but the message of this book goes far beyond us.

OUR BATTLES

As I've shared with other people my story of having an affair, I've learned about their battles. Chances are, you're fighting some of these battles too. Are you:

- Addicted to porn, alcohol, drugs, or food?

- Having an affair?

- In a bad marriage?

- Suffering from broken relationships with family members?

- Looking to others for approval?

- Feeling insecure and alone?

- Still suffering from wounds of the past?

- Comparing yourself to others?

- Feeling like you don't do enough?

- Laying your head on the pillow at night and thinking you will never catch up?

- Striving to reach the top of the corporate ladder so you can feel better about yourself?

Maybe you're successful on the outside, crushing it at work, but not at home and not personally. You know you're not living life to the full, and it tears you apart.

Before I came clean about my affair, I was trying to offset the defeat I was feeling in my personal life with wins at work. I thought, *I know I'm not winning at home, but if I can win at work, I will be OK.* Truth is, the math does not work like that. It is not a zero-sum game. Personal life counts so much more than professional life.

PUTTING IT ALL TOGETHER

After I came clean about my affair, I still didn't know how to fix my situation. I didn't have any tools. I was desperate. How do I avoid falling into this trap again? What if I don't have an affair, but I have another personal failure? How do I succeed personally with all the work demands? How do I make sure I have the right priorities? Plus, God said I was supposed to hand over my story for a greater story. What is the greater story?

During this time, I was promoted, and we transferred to Cincinnati and found an incredible church called Crossroads. After a few weeks of attending Crossroads, I volunteered in the Kids' Club giving tours of the children's ministry. Crossroads was planning to undergo a two-year immersion program where they would learn about discipleship from a faith-based leadership development company called 3DM. The plan was for Crossroads to send fifty staff members and fifty volunteers through this two-year program that would meet quarterly. After just a few weeks of volunteering, I met Kim Botto, who at the time was responsible for Kids' Club at Crossroads. For some reason Kim Botto submitted my name to be one of the fifty volunteers. At the time Crossroads was a 10,000-person church, so being selected was all God's doing.

This two-year immersion was an incredible experience as I learned tools that brought the Bible to life and was provided tools to apply in my personal life. During the last session of this two-year immersion, they divided the group into different rooms based on where each person wanted to implement these ideas, such as family, business, or church.

I chose the "business" room and absolutely loved the session! I learned how to take these tools we learned over the past two years and integrate them with business books like *Good to Great*, *The Five Dysfunctions of a Team*, and others. Afterwards I went up to the 3DM facilitator, Brandon Schaefer, who is now

Executive Director of Five Capitals, an international coaching and consulting company. I told him I loved it and wanted to learn more. He told me he did executive coaching, and so our relationship began!

At the time I was a VP of a $100 million division at Contech, a site solutions provider in the civil engineering market, and I needed help. My boss was a great guy and I learned a lot from him, but unfortunately, we didn't spend enough time together due to our travels. Plus, I wanted to learn how to integrate my faith better into all areas of my life, and I knew Brandon could help me with that.

COACH BRANDON . . . AND COACH CORY

With Brandon as my executive coach, I started implementing all these tools and others I learned along the way. I shared them with my direct reports at work. I used them with my family as well as some friends. I started to see improvement in myself and others.

In my next corporate job, I was president of sales for a national contractor and had thirty sales representatives reporting to me. I used all of these coaching tools with them. If they believed in Jesus, I'd say, "Jesus said . . . ," and provide the applicable verse and the accompanying tool to help the employee with their need in that moment. If they were not a believer, I'd say, "Steve Jobs said . . . ," and found a similar quote and then used the same tool. Not that Jesus and Steve Jobs are the same guy, but all truth is God's truth and resonates regardless of the source.

These tools certainly made me a better leader, but they also made me a better husband, father, and friend. After using these tools with employees and others, I saw transformation! I found people going after purpose instead of a paycheck, starting to date their spouses again, thinking through work/life balance better, being more intentional with their kids, and the list goes on.

After seeing transformation not only in my own life but also in the lives of the thirty employees who reported to me, God put it in my heart to share the message further. This was the greater story—leaving my job in corporate America so I could share these tools with many more people.

I did just that. I left corporate America as an employee to become a coach to corporate America. To show others there is a better way and the tools and insights to help guide them. The last few years as an executive coach have confirmed there is a need in the workplace, and the tools in this book really do work. Just look at what some of my clients have said:

"Cory has a unique gift of combining keen discernment, practical wisdom, and personal relatability to ignite true progress. His approach comes from an angle not of coach to student, but person-to-person. The time I spent with Cory impacted my leadership not only at work, but even more importantly in my role as a husband and father."
Nick Spicher
Business Unit Director, Harvest Group

"I've worked with a lot of coaches, and Cory is the best. He has focused on my personal growth over my professional growth, and what I've found is that when you grow personally, you always grow professionally, but not necessarily the other way around. In a world where coaches only pay lip service to personal growth, Cory stands out. He has made me not only a better businessman, but a better man."
Ben Beshear
Wealth Management Advisor and Managing Director,
Northwestern Mutual

"As with many coaching relationships, mine began with Cory at a pivotal time in my career, when I was assessing whether to pivot and go a different direction or stay true to my calling. Some coaches coach from making statements. But great coaches ask great questions to lead to a process of self-discovery. That's what happened with Cory over the course of a year in coaching with him. I can't recommend his care and candor enough. Cory is a leader in his own right and gives excellent coaching to other leaders. He asks great questions and leads great discussions. My life, family, and organization are better because of time spent in coaching with Cory."

Jeremy Self

Pastor, The Church at Lake Travis

"Since I partnered with Cory, my whole life has changed, and only for the better. The work we have done together has been incredible. My personal and professional life has been enriched through this process. Working with Cory changed the way I look and think about every situation. I am 100 percent a better person inside and out. I would implore anyone who has the opportunity to work with Cory to grab it with both hands—you won't be sorry."

Peter Lane

Marketing Manager, Johnson & Johnson

"I am grateful we hired Cory and for the lasting impact his coaching has had on our team. His passion and personality blended with his direct approach and real-world experience provide a great environment for transformation and growth. Plus, the tools and concepts he uses can be used at all levels and are great for teaching across the entire organization."

Chris Hendriksen

Chairman of VRI

"Thank you for being such a great support over this past year. I can't thank you enough for helping me grow and become a stronger leader."

Carolina Farfan

Marketing Manager, Johnson & Johnson

"Cory Carlson is an accomplished executive coach as he prompts a metamorphosis in business leaders through the Five Capitals principles, increasing an individual's impact at both work and home. His blend of character, business acumen, and sensitivity are what business leaders need today. I have hired Cory to coach five of our top leaders at the bank, as well as lead our new Leadership Development program, an ongoing annual commitment to groom leaders from within our own ranks. I would confidently recommend Cory to any business owner looking to increase the impact and depth of their business leaders."

Chris Caddell

Chairman of Heritage Bank

WHY I WROTE THIS BOOK

As I have been coaching business leaders and executives for the last few years, I have been surprised by a consistent theme. Yes, they want to be financially successful. Yes, they want to grow. Yes, they want to build a great team. But I've noticed again and again these business leaders are concerned most about how to get their personal life in order. How to get themselves and their homes right.

You cannot give your best at work if you are always thinking about how to patch things up at home. There is a better way. This book distills the tools and concepts that have helped not only my transformation but hundreds of others.

Does that mean you won't have arguments with your spouse after reading this book? Your kids won't ever get in trouble? Absolutely not. But this book provides insights and ideas for build-ing a stronger personal foundation built on character, not just competency.

Many of us know we need God at the center of our lives. The secret is not just to say God is at the center. The secret is not to start going to church on Sunday and then operate your own way the rest of the week. The secret is not to start saying a prayer at dinner time in front of others and not have prayer in solitude. Yes, we need to have God at the center of our lives, but it has to be in action, not just intention.

I love this quote from Steve Maraboli: "An inch of action will take you closer to your goals than a mile of intention." We can't just intend to have God at the center; instead, we need to take action. By taking action and putting God in all aspects of life, we can succeed at home and work.

LET'S GET STARTED!

PART 1

YOU

"But when one turns to the Lord, the veil is removed. Now the Lord is the Spirit, and where the Spirit of the Lord is, there is freedom. And we all, with unveiled face, beholding the glory of the Lord, are being transformed into the same image from one degree of glory to another. For this comes from the Lord who is the Spirit."

2 Corinthians 3:16–18

"If I really want to improve my situation, I can work on the one thing over which I have control—myself."

STEVEN COVEY
The 7 Habits of Highly Effective People

1

WHO ARE YOU?

Discovering the Best Place to Form Our Identity

I heard former Navy SEAL Chad Williams tell his incredible story a couple years ago. Although I as a businessman can't relate to many of Chad's war stories, the battle with our identity tied to our success or failure is one we all can relate to.

Throughout Chad's journey he tied his identity to the accomplishment right in front of him. Chad struggled in school, eventually dropping out of junior college. People started to tell him he wasn't good enough, so that became his identity—a failure. Luckily a family friend, Scott Helvenston, was a Navy SEAL and saw something different in Chad. Scott took Chad under his wing and prepared him mentally and physically for SEAL training.

Days prior to entering SEAL training, Chad unexpectedly saw a graphic video of Scott being brutally killed in Iraq. This tragic event caused Chad to shift his identity to not only being a Navy SEAL but being the best in honor and memory of Scott.

Chad inscribed Scott's name inside his hat as a reminder of what he was fighting for. His identity was to become a Navy SEAL, and he pushed forward, eventually graduating as one of 13 Navy SEALS out of a class of 173 men who tried out. However, when he received his graduation pin, it wasn't enough. Something was missing, and it wasn't just his friend Scott. Instead it was internal.

Chad had tied his identity to that of a Navy SEAL, and when he accomplished the feat, it felt empty. The hole in his heart he was trying to fill was still void. The destination of the pursuit was not fulfilling. Instead of feeling on top of the world, he felt lost. Chad began a downward spiral of alcoholism, bar fights, and other bad choices.

Over the years I've worked with numerous clients who, like Chad, are looking for fulfillment in the wrong places:

- a corner-office executive who doesn't know his children

- a pastor who is more concerned about congregation size than helping people follow Jesus

- a mom who yells at her children for making messes because she wants the house to always be spotless

- a husband and wife both trying to advance in their careers but haven't been on a date in months

- a dad who travels, proud to say he rarely misses his kids' games, yet the only time he does see his children is from the bleachers

- an athlete who has a career-ending injury and doesn't know who she is now

- a woman who counts every calorie, thinking it will bring happiness

Maybe you are experiencing this right now. A sense of wandering, a sense of being lost.

- Do you feel like your ladder is leaning against the wrong building?

- Is your life as fulfilling as you thought it would be?

- Are your priorities in the right order?

- Are the people closest to you getting the best version of you?

- Are you securing your identity through temporary pursuits?

- Is work currently more important than your spouse? Kids? Physical health? Spirituality?

- Are you making first things second and second things first?

- Do you ever feel you are pursuing a lifestyle, an accomplishment, a dream that is to be the answer to your questions about yourself and life?

- Do you ever feel you are putting your eggs in the wrong basket?

- Do you ever ask God for help in the small decisions, or do you just call on Him when you are in panic mode?

- Are you successful in a worldly sense but still feel insignificant?

If any of these questions resonate, the great news is there is a better way. Keep reading!

KNOW YOURSELF

Before you can lead well at home or work, you have to know yourself.

Brandon Schaefer, my executive coach for years, says, "You have to know yourself, so you can forget yourself, so that you can freely give yourself." Unpacking that idea, if you truly know who you are, what you stand for, and what you are going after, you can forget your imposter-self, your selfish desires, your insecurities, your fears, your doubts, your cares of what others think of you. And you can actually "give yourself away," in other words, be present with people. Actually listening to people talk instead of waiting to talk. Thinking about how you can serve others instead of the other way around.

If you do not understand who you are, you will always be looking in other places for the answer. You will take your questions of identity and self-worth to your job or your spouse or another man or woman. You may look to the success of your kids. You may even take your questions to coping mechanisms like alcohol, TV, or porn.

None of these places will provide a sustainable and life-giving answer. If you take your questions to your job and you do not get the promotion, or you get fired, how will you view yourself? If you take your questions to your spouse, what if he or she is having a bad day and does not give you the answer you want? What if your kids don't make the sports team or drop out of college?

When we take our questions to temporal things, we are building an identity on very sandy soil. Instead, we need to understand that our identity is in being a beloved son or daughter of God.

WHAT GOD THINKS OF US

One of my absolute favorite teachings on identity is taught by The New Frontier, a ministry founded by my friend and mentor Chris Hartenstein, who helps people better understand their true identity as a beloved son or daughter of God. This ministry has weeklong immersions in Montana, helping people process four main life questions, one of which is, "Who am I?"

One of the activities we do in Montana is going on a three-mile hike to the top of Bear Creek Overlook. When we get to the top, the view is majestic.

Imagine standing on a mountaintop in western Montana. You can see for miles. You see mountain ranges all around you, even into Idaho. Standing on top of Bear Creek Overlook, you also can look over Bitterroot Valley and to the Sapphire Mountains on the other side of the valley. You see the beautiful yellow tamarack trees spread up and down the mountainsides, mixed in with the green ponderosa pines and evergreens. Looking directly down you can faintly see Bear Creek flowing below.

Now Chris pulls everybody together and tells you to look around and say words to describe what you see. "Awesome," says somebody to your left, just as someone in front of you says, "Beautiful." "Epic." "Unbelievable." People throw out words like this for some time. You toss in some of your own.

Chris looks at all of you and reminds you that after God created this mountain range, and all the other beautiful parts of the world, Genesis tells us that on the fifth day, God called it "Good." Yet when He created man and woman on the sixth day, God said, "Very Good."

Even in all of our brokenness, weaknesses, and quirks, we are "Very Good." With that in mind, we can start walking in confidence that we are loved as a beloved son or daughter of God.

MY STORY

In my twenties and early thirties, I tied my identity to my wins at work. The amount of money I made, my title, and the speed I was climbing the corporate ladder. This journey led to seeking approval from others, whether it was my affair mentioned earlier, making foolish moves to make additional money in real estate, or other unwise endeavors.

Fortunately, in my early thirties I started to shift my identity from that of a businessman to a beloved son of God. A critical quote I learned on my identity journey was from Mike Breen, founder of 3DM: "You are working *from* a place of approval, instead of *for* approval." That perspective was a game changer for me! Instead of looking to others for approval, we are already approved by God!

On August 15, 2016, I was terminated from my highest salary, biggest job title, and most significant corporate responsibility to date. The three years leading up to that day, I was president of sales for a national contractor, and the journey was an incredible experience. But at the direction of our private equity owners, we significantly downsized our footprint, which eliminated the need for my role. The old me would have been devastated. Crushed. Instead, I felt freedom. I took the job loss as clarity for what God had in store for me.

BACK TO THE NAVY SEAL

While Chad Williams was at the bottom of his life, he tells the story of sneaking back into his parents' house to get a keg he had left there a few days prior because he was needing a fix.

While there, he ran into his parents, who invited him to church that night. Feeling deep longing for a better way, he agreed to go.

Attending church that night was life-changing for Chad. He realized there was a greater story. He realized he was no longer defined by his achievements of being a top-tier Navy SEAL or by his brokenness as an alcoholic. From that point forward Chad's story has been one of restoration as well as living into his identity as a beloved son. Chad went on to write his inspirational memoir *SEAL of God* and shares his amazing testimony of restoration with thousands as he speaks across the country.

RECALIBRATION QUESTIONS

As we come to grips with our identity and getting better at taking our questions to God through prayer, Scripture, solitude, and journaling, we can start to better understand ourselves. I wish I would have figured this out sooner. I am not perfect today, and I still have struggles, but I am much quicker to recalibrate and get my identity and values more aligned with God. As Paul says in 2 Corinthians 3:18, we are all getting closer one degree at a time.

At the end of each chapter in this book, there will be recalibration questions to help you recalibrate and better align your heart and mind with God's character. I encourage you to take the time to answer these questions to help bring transformation and growth.

1. What do you tie your identity to? Is it in the temporal things of your life—your job, your marriage, your kids, your health, your finances?

2. Is your identity tied to a destination or accomplishment?

3. Is your identity still being tied to a past failure? Is it tied to a business or marriage that failed?

4. Is your identity tied to eternal things such as being a beloved son or daughter of God?

5. How can you shift your mindset to be more focused on being a child of God?

2

WHERE ARE YOU GOING?

We Need to Know What We Are Pursuing

The other day my daughter was invited to a birthday party at a brand-new, indoor trampoline park. I had heard of these cool parks but had not been, nor did I know how to get there. I grabbed the birthday invitation, jumped in the car with my kids, pulled up the GPS app on my phone, and typed in the destination.

A popup appeared requesting permission to know my current location. Once the phone knew where I was, it was able to provide directions.

Our life is the same way. We need to know our current location, not only who we are in Christ but if we are truly living as His child, before we can move forward. Once we've established our identity as God's beloved, we can begin plotting our route forward.

Y VISION EVOLUTION

My wife and I joke that she has been married to one husband t a few different men. My personal vision kept changing ear- r in our marriage because my vision was small and tied only my job. When I was a civil engineer, I defined myself as that; only vision for my life was to be CEO of that firm. On days I ought I was progressing toward that vision, I felt satisfied; on ys I didn't feel progress or maybe even had a setback because a project didn't go well, I was crushed. I questioned who I was and where was I going.

When I moved into sales, my vision was to be the best sales person and eventually be the CEO of that company or another engineering products company. Once again, my identity would go up and down based on the type of day I had. When I became president of sales for the national contractor, we were owned by a private equity group, and my vision was to be their go-to CEO in future acquisitions.

What is the vision for your life? Is your vision tied to your current job? Does your vision include others outside of your work?

As mentioned earlier, my vision changed after I hired an executive coach. After seeing this transformation in my life and in others' lives, God put on my heart my new vision, the one I still live with today:

> *To connect people to greater performance, and even more significant purpose.*

I have experienced such freedom in having a vision for my life. Having a vision greater than a job title or role means it applies anywhere and everywhere. Whether I work for a small company or big company, I know I am to be connecting people to greater performance and trying to help them live into a more significant purpose. Whether I am in my neighborhood or volunteering at my kids' school, I know I am called to help people think about ways to live life to the full.

For me, more significant purpose for others looks like improving a daily walk with Jesus Christ. However, for my clients who do not believe in God or Jesus, I still see growth because they start to believe in something greater than themselves.

YOUR TURN

What is your personal vision statement? We work with clients to better define their current location and their perspective, and from there we help them build out their priorities in order to reach their desired potential.

Claiming our identity as a beloved son or daughter is just part of the perspective and identity piece. Combining this with our life story and how we are uniquely wired helps us complete the picture. Our achievements, wounds, and experiences are what make us unique. As Chris Hartenstein says, "You can't truly know someone until you know their story."

Below is a framework called 5Ps that we use with clients to help give guidance in creating their vision statement. The 5Ps are passions, provision, problems, personality, and potential. These 5Ps will help you to not only see how you are uniquely made, but also proclaim your story and testimony.

Spend some time answering the questions in each of the five areas and then construct a vision statement sentence that gets you emotional. That's right, emotional! The goal is to come up with a vision statement you are so passionate about that when you say it out loud the first few times, your voice cracks.

I encourage you to think about this at different times and places, such as in the morning over coffee during your journaling time, during an afternoon walk outside, or in the evening with a nightcap. Once you answer the questions, what you choose to use in your statement and the order in which you put them is up to you. We have found that using the 5Ps provides enough of a framework to identify words and phrases that speak to your heart. I encourage you to complete all 5Ps, but as you can see from my example and the examples below, not all the Ps make it to the final vision statement. This is just a guide you can customize to fit your calling. Freedom within the framework.

PASSIONS

Chad Allen was my writing coach on the front end of this project and helped with the developmental edit. I found him via a referral from friend and author Todd Henry. Todd told me Chad was passionate about helping writers get their message to the market. I believed Todd but was also curious if that was really true. I experienced this in my first phone call with Chad. He was more interested in learning about my book than selling me his services. He asked a lot of thoughtful and caring questions. Why did I want to write the book? Who was my intended audience? How would this help them? How did I get to the point of wanting to write a book? What would happen if this book was never written? He even asked questions about me and my family.

Chad's curiosity was to better understand me and my message and think through how to get it across the finish line. I could tell in our first phone call that he wasn't just interested in cranking through the editing process to collect his monthly payment. I could tell he not only wanted to edit my book, but he wanted to be a part of the journey.

During the writing process he demonstrated this partnership mentality even more. Our calls always went longer than planned, and he provided edits throughout the month that he probably didn't budget for. Since Chad cared for the project and me, he invested more time. His passion is to help people create something better than they could on their own.

Chad Allen's personal vision statement is:

I feel deeply called to help creative people do their best work.

I believe he's doing just that.

PASSION QUESTIONS

What gets you excited? What fires you up? What gives you energy? What do you love to do? List all your passions. Just keep writing them down. Do you like spending time with people? Do you like solving problems? Do you like to be creative? Do you like to write? Speak? Do you like coming up with new ideas or implementing somebody else's?

Passion is often motivated by love. Maybe there is an area where you have been broken and you are passionate about helping people in that area.

Take some time now to journal about your passions. Use the space below to capture your thoughts and answer the above questions.

_____

_____

_____

_____

_____

_____

PROVISION

A great friend of mine, Ray Bonomo, is one of the most generous people I know. He makes a good living as a periodontist, but his generosity is not a function of how much money he makes. His generosity is a mindset. It is who he is.

A few summers ago, another friend of mine, Tony, and I were building a pergola in my backyard. (Truth be told, Tony did all the work since I am not very handy!) Ray thought it would be fun to get the rest of our men's Bible study group together that night at my house so we could hang out as well as see the construction progress.

Instead of just ordering pizza or something simple, Ray loaded up his car and brought over his smoker and meat from a recent hunting trip that he was willing to share with all of us. As if that weren't enough, Ray also brought over wine and side dishes.

Ray's generosity went beyond just providing all the equipment and food. Because he wanted to be at my house so everyone could see the construction project taking place, he invested a lot of time bringing everything to my house instead of having us over to his house. His generosity also included cooking and serving us, instead of someone else working the grill.

When Ray and I worked together in a coaching/client engagement and came to his personal vision statement, he was frustrated because he didn't have one. He longed for a vision statement but didn't know where to start. As we worked through the process, all he could think of was "Pour yourself out." It was a phrase he felt God placed on his heart. He was excited because the statement started to clarify things in his life. The vision statement gave Ray a new filter through which to view the stresses of his job, his commitments, and his family.

Ray Bonomo's personal vision statement is:

Pour yourself out.

As a friend, and his past coach, I think he truly lives this out.

PROVISION QUESTIONS

What has God provided for you in your life? Relationships, material possessions, accolades, and more. What is God currently providing you? New opportunities, new relationships? Where has God been working in your life? What has God uniquely provided you? Do you have a college education? Are you doing something you love? Do certain accomplishments tell your story? Where has there been grace and favor in your life?

Assessing the provisions in your life shows you where God has been at work in your life. When we see God's provision, we see how much was out of our control and actually provided by God's amazing grace and mercy. Once we see where God has provided in the past, as well as areas he is currently providing, it gives us hope to dream, knowing He has provided before and will again.

Take some time now to journal about God's provision in your life. Use the space below to capture your thoughts and answer the above questions.

_____

_____

_____

_____

_____

_____

_____

PROBLEMS

In September 2017, I was hired by Missy Bricking for executive coaching and development of her real estate team. Missy is a very successful realtor who owns Missy B Realty Group at Keller Williams in the Greater Cincinnati Tri-State Area, and I was impressed with the drive and enthusiasm she had when we met.

In the early stages of coaching engagements, I work with clients to identify the key moments in their story. From our key moments, we can see how God is molding us, especially when we allow Him to do His work. A key part of Missy's story is being a single mom of an eight-year-old boy. Missy's tension is between being a successful realtor and business owner and being a successful mom. She is successful at both, but it takes intentionality, accountability, and many sacrifices.

She has realized many women are in this same situation yet are not having success balancing the two. Some of these women feel alone and don't know where to go for help. Missy began helping single moms find success at home and work and overcome this problem. She hired a single mom on her team and is working with her not only in growing their business but in helping her be successful outside work as well. She also started a single moms group on Facebook to help build a community for these women, so they can get tips and support along the way. She also leads a single moms group at her local church.

Missy's personal vision is one she lives
out by serving single moms:

*Devoted to servicing our clients' real estate needs
at a high level to help our clients and our team
build a LEGACY for themselves and their family
while creating life-long relationships.*

PROBLEM QUESTIONS

What is a problem you overcame that you want to help others overcome? What has been a roadblock in your life, but no longer is? What do you want to solve today? This year? Is there an addiction that you want to put a stop to?

Problems are motivated by brokenness, whether it is yours directly or something you see around you. Recently I talked with a woman who struggled with an eating disorder for more than twenty years, so she wants to empower women, especially teenage girls, to better understand their value and worth so they do not tie it to their outward appearance.

Take some time now to journal about the problems in your life that you have overcome. Use the space below to capture your thoughts and answer the above questions.

_____

_____

_____

_____

_____

PERSONALITY

The other day I was invited to a restaurant for 1:30 p.m. meeting with Ron Beshear, a retired managing partner with Northwestern Mutual in Cincinnati. Ron has had a very successful business career not only because of his business acumen but because of the relationships he established along the way. People know he is more about relationship than transaction.

When I got to the restaurant for our meeting, he was finishing up another meeting, and he invited me to sit down next to him. I felt like I was intruding, but this was not an accident. Ron wanted both of his guests to meet and purposely overlapped the meetings.

Ron Beshear is a connector. Yes, he is an extrovert and loves spending time with people, but he is more about connecting people to each other for the benefit of all. When Ron invites me to something, I have no idea what to expect, other than it will be a great chance to meet more of his network.

I first met Ron when a mutual friend introduced us. Shortly after that introduction, Ron attended one of my live events. Ron has seen many live events in his lifetime, read many books and even wrote one, and can deliver a great message himself, but I noticed he diligently took notes during my presentation. I later found out he took notes not only because he is lifelong learner, but because Ron knew the better he understood my content and my heart, the better he would be able to promote me and my coaching. Since then Ron has introduced me to numerous people and hosted multiple events where he invited other business leaders.

Ron's vision is to serve people by connecting them to others, all to expand their purpose. Ron executes his vision so well:

Serving your purpose.

He lives out this vision through a nonprofit by that name (www.servingyourpurpose.com).

PERSONALITY QUESTIONS

How are you wired? Are you an extrovert or introvert? A thinker or a doer? A visionary or implementer? A pioneer or settler? If you want to go deeper here, I recommend a personality assessment through DISC, the Enneagram, or Myers-Briggs (go to www.winathomefirstbook.com/resources if you need an assessment). Personality is also about what gives you energy. We are all wired to do certain tasks, and when we do them, they bring us life. Whereas, if we are not doing them, they are draining.

Take some time now to journal about what makes you unique by your personality. Use the space below to capture your thoughts and answer the above questions.

_____

_____

_____

_____

_____

POTENTIAL

I am blessed to be on the board of directors of an incredible nonprofit, Aruna, which provides sustainable employment to women freed from sex slavery. How this nonprofit started was a direct result of somebody changing the trajectory of his life not only because of a problem he wanted to solve, but the potential he saw in the solution.

Ryan Berg, founder of Aruna, was part of Campus Crusade for Christ (CRU), a ministry for college students. Part of his job at CRU was to find a project off-campus, even outside the country if possible, to get the college students involved in expanding God's Kingdom in the world.

Ryan was in a season of discovery and praying about where to take the ministry when he saw the ticker running across the bottom of a CNN newscast that changed his life. The statistic was the number of women who were sex trafficked in Mumbai, India. Ryan was shocked by the numbers. How could it be? How could something that awful take place in this world? Was anybody trying to stop it?

Ryan could not stop thinking about the statistic, so he decided to take steps to learn more. He started asking questions, met with people, and read anything he could find about sex trafficking in India. Then he traveled to India and explored starting a nonprofit.

Eight years after seeing the statistic on CNN, Ryan and April Berg are making a difference. They resigned from CRU and started Aruna, an athleisure lifestyle brand that combines the best of nonprofit and for profit to bring lifelong freedom to the enslaved. Today, seventeen running races across the United States raise money and awareness for Aruna, while the business continues to produce functional luxury athleisure accessories. In its short four-year life, Aruna has employed fifty-three women in Mumbai, where each woman earns a living wage, retirement benefits, and health care all wrapped in a community of holistic care.

Ryan has a God-sized vision for the potential of his nonprofit and business. In what seems like a battle without a victory due to the amount of sex trafficking in this world, Ryan is committed to do what he can. His vision is to employ thousands of women, provide housing and holistic care, and eventually move to other parts of the world to continue to employ women! Ryan has a bigger vision than what he can do alone.

Ryan Berg's vision statement is one he lives out daily:

Provide sustainable employment to women
freed from sex trafficking.

POTENTIAL QUESTIONS

We need to have a vision for ourselves that is built on something greater than temporary achievements and actions. We need a vision that will apply to our life, both at work and at home. A vision that is bigger than ourselves. A vision that is God-dependent and not self-dependent.

What do you want to be known for? What legacy are you building? We have heard the question, "Are you building your life for your resume or your obituary?" Your resume is more about you. Your obituary is more about a lasting impact on others. Or try this: Imagine talking to your future self, lying on your death bed. What would your future self tell you about what you need to do?

Take some time now to journal about what makes you unique by your potential. Use the space below to capture your thoughts and answer the above questions.

_____

_____

_____

_____

_____

_____

_____

NOW IT'S YOUR TURN!

Without a vision statement, we drift and wander, so use the bottom of this page to start drafting some ideas for your vision statement. 1, 2, 3 . . . Go!

_____

_____

_____

_____

_____

_____

_____

_____

3

THE FIVE CAPITALS

We Need to Know How to Live a Prioritized Life

Congratulations on completing your vision statement! Now that you know where you are going, we need to determine how to get you there. Keeping the GPS metaphor in mind, your current location is where you are today. Your destination is your vision statement. And now we turn to the directions to your destination: how we do life to live out our vision statement.

When you drive to a destination, you need to know when to turn left or right, when to speed up or slow down. Our lives are very similar. Sometimes we need to turn and go a different direction because an opportunity is no longer available. Or we need to recalibrate and stop habits that get out of whack. Other times we need to accelerate in order to get some things done.

And then at times we need to slow down, rest, and relax.

The following chapters cover disciplines needed for growth. It is one thing to believe a new identity and vision; it is altogether different to live it out. Similarly, reading this book is easy. But when we hit the matrix on Monday and all the demands of work, we can easily go back to our old ways. Our old ways of striving, looking to others for approval, self-dependence, comparing our lives to others.

THE FIVE CAPITALS

The fact that I left my corporate career to pursue coaching is a major testament to the effectiveness of the five capitals framework. This is foundational to the executive coaching I received as well as what I provide business leaders today.

In John 10:10 Jesus said, "I came that they may have life and have it abundantly." He came to give life, life to the full. When we look around, though, our lives can feel chaotic. Running from meeting to meeting, phone call to phone call, and email to email. If we are not careful, it can start to feel like everything is important so that, really, *nothing* is important. The demands of the moment can end up overriding our long-term purpose. We let the impulse of today be more important than an investment for tomorrow.

The five capitals are based on two parables found in Matthew 25 and Luke 16. In Matthew 25:14–30, the Parable of the Talents, a master gives talents to three different servants. For context, a talent was worth about twenty years' wages for a laborer. So in today's dollars, if the annual median personal income is about $31,000 (per the U.S Census Bureau for 2016), one talent then is equivalent to $620,000 today! That is serious money. In today's dollars, one servant got $3.1 million, another servant got $1.2 million, and the other servant got $620 thousand. The master was truly empowering his servants! The servants who received five and two talents went and doubled their money. When the master came back, he was ecstatic and said, "Well done, good and faithful servants!"

But the master was not as pleased with the third servant. The third servant, as Scripture says in Matthew 25:25, "was afraid," and he chose to bury the talent because he did not want to lose the money. The master calls him a "wicked and slothful servant!" Ouch! Our first thought is, "How harsh is that!" But that is the kind of God and Father we have—one who gives lavishly yet wants a return on His investment.

Guess who the investment is? You are. I am. We are called to take our time, talent, and treasures and invest them and get a return. The experiences and testimony we have, the wisdom we have gained, the restoration from our failures, our story—all of this needs to be shared to help others grow and give God and the Kingdom a return on His investment. If you are learning but not teaching and sharing with others, you are burying your treasure. If you are sitting on insight and ideas but not taking action due to fear, you are being "wicked." We need to be investing not only into ourselves but also into our families, friends, and those who work for us.

Next parable. In Luke 16:1–13, a general manager knows the owner is about to fire him. As the general manager is thinking about what to do next, he realizes he is "not strong enough to dig" (physical capital) and "ashamed to beg." The general manager has an idea (intellectual capital) to negotiate with the current customers. He begins asking customers how much they owe. One customer owes a hundred measures of oil, and the general manager reduces the debt to fifty measures. He asks the next customer what he owes—a hundred measures of wheat, which he reduces to eighty.

What does the owner say when he returns? Is he angry at the manager for reducing debts? Not at all. Instead, the owner is pleased because the general manager leverages a lower capital (financial capital) for a greater capital (relational capital). The purpose of this parable is to encourage us to leverage our different capitals for greater gain for the Kingdom. In this parable, money is not the end all, be all. Jesus actually ends this parable in Luke 16:13, with, "No servant can serve two masters, for either he will hate the one and love the other, or he will be devoted to the one and despise the other. You cannot serve God and money."

As Brandon Schaefer states in *Build a Better Life*, "Jesus is saying it is worth investing your financial capital to grow your relational capital, because relational capital is worth far more than financial capital."

These two parables together show there are different capitals in our life, and we are charged with leveraging them in such a way that we bring a return on investment to God.

WHAT ARE THE FIVE CAPITALS?

The following is an overview of the five capitals in order of priority. For a more detailed discussion of the five capitals, visit www.winathomefirstbook.com/resources.

- **SPIRITUAL:** This capital has to do with our relationship with God. The greatest command is to love God. It's the most valuable of the capitals and is measured in wisdom.

- **RELATIONAL:** This capital is about the relational equity (or trust) we've built up (or eroded) with others. The second greatest command is to love others. The relational capital is about both the quality and depth of our relationships. It's measured in influence and impact.

- **PHYSICAL:** The physical capital relates to the time and energy we have available to invest in other people. Time is the great equalizer. We have one life to make the most of. This capital is measured in hours and minutes.

- **INTELLECTUAL:** This capital refers to our creativity and knowledge. The skills and competences we learn allow us to thrive in life. It's measured in insight and ideas.

- **FINANCIAL:** Finally, the financial capital relates to money, tangible resources we have available to invest. It's about stewarding all the resources we have and is measured in dollars and cents.

The following chapters provide practices to help you grow in each of these capitals.

4

SPIRITUAL CAPITAL

What Is God Telling You?

Recently I went on a spiritual retreat with a heaviness over me. A feeling of defeat. A feeling of not being capable. Of not being good enough.

In order to hit some goals for my coaching business, I had some big actions I wanted to take. I needed to increase my audience significantly, which felt daunting. I was on the hunt for new leadership teams to coach, not just one-on-one engagements but teams. I wanted to build out content packages on my website to deepen my level of service. I needed to increase my speaking engagements to help get the message out.

I had this enormous feeling of being overwhelmed, which was leading to fear and doubt.

As I sat in my chair, I started writing questions down and taking my fears to God. *What if I have events and nobody shows up? If I can't find new clients, what am I going to do financially? This book seems to be a God idea, not just my idea, but where are the resources to make it happen?*

At the top of the next page I wrote, "Lord, where do I not have faith? Why do I not have faith? God, where am I not 'all in'?"

I started writing as fast as I could different reasons and excuses for answers to all those questions. The main theme I saw was a scarcity mindset. I even wrote, "If I'm honest, I feel that all I get is 'just enough' resources, yet I see others with more abundance."

Then out of nowhere I heard, "*Look how far I have come.*" I wrote it down and stared. What? How could I go from feeling defeated to all of a sudden feeling grateful for how far I have come? That message must have come from God.

Then I sensed God leading me to consider all the new relationships and experiences I'd had in the previous two years since leaving corporate America. I wrote down all the clients, experiences, and events that came to mind. Looking at the lists of clients, I realized I didn't even know the majority of them when I began coaching! God brought new relationships into my life.

The list of experiences was wild: leading a women's retreat, involvement in The New Frontier ministry, leading retreats and sessions with Ocean (a top accelerator in the country for small businesses integrating faith and business), participating in the Leadership section of Venue magazine—all of these were new adventures God created!

Here's my point. God had something to tell me, but if I hadn't taken the time to listen, I would have missed it. I would have continued in a mindset of doubt and fear and trying to overcome it with my own effort.

WHAT IS SPIRITUAL CAPITAL?

Spiritual capital is our relationship with God. From our relationship with God we understand our identity. We receive wisdom on the actions to take. We get clarity on who we are and where we are going.

In order to grow in our relationship with God, we need to spend time with Him. Jesus modeled this for us. The Bible records several times when Jesus went to be alone with His Father, but one verse I particularly like is Mark 1:35, "And rising very early in the morning, while it was still dark, he departed and went out to a desolate place, and there he prayed." After a very busy day of healing the sick and casting out demons, He rose up very early in the morning and went off by Himself and prayed.

In verse 37, some of His disciples found Him and were concerned, maybe even frustrated, that He was gone. "Everyone is looking for you," they said. People were looking for Jesus because they wanted more of Him. People wanted more healings, more demons cast out, more teachings. People wanted to see what Jesus was going to do next. Jesus was on a roll, and people wanted to see the show.

Yet Jesus knew He could not keep doing these miracles without hitting pause and reconnecting with His Father. Not only did He reconnect and get rest, He actually got redirected. When Jesus responded to them in verse 38, He said, "Let us go on to the next towns, that I may preach there also, for that is why I came out." Jesus was not meant to stand in the same place and have a single-file line of sick and demon-possessed people come to Him. Instead He was to go to various cities and teach, as well as heal. Jesus got this insight from His time of solitude. He knew He would not hear God's voice in the busyness of the day.

The devil loves busyness because it keeps us away from spending time with our Father. When I am on a roll, I want to keep going. I don't want the momentum to stop. Unlike Jesus, I can tend to think I am so busy I don't have time to connect with God.

How often do we feel the pull on our time?

- Our kids constantly need our help—take them to this activity and then to that activity.

- Emails never stop coming in for work.

- The client is not happy and keeps calling.

- The boss continues to text and wants answers.

- Sales are going well, so we want to keep going and strike while the iron is hot.

- Or sales are slow, so we need to get out there and make our numbers.

Jesus knew busyness and resisting dependence on God would be a problem for us. That is why He talked about it a few different times. One of my favorites is the Sermon on the Mount.

In this teaching Jesus shares a lot of wisdom, some of which is so popular that people who aren't even familiar with the Bible have heard of it. For example: "Love your neighbor," and, "You can't love God and money." Most interesting to me is that Jesus ends this famous talk with a story about "The Wise Builder" (Matthew 7:24–27). In order to be a wise builder, Jesus teaches, you need to hear His words and do them, whereas the foolish man does not hear the words and does not do them.

Five Capitals, the coaching and consulting organization I work with, developed the Hearing and Doing Matrix as a way to help people visualize this teaching. Following are brief descriptions of each quadrant. *Hearing* is having the humility to

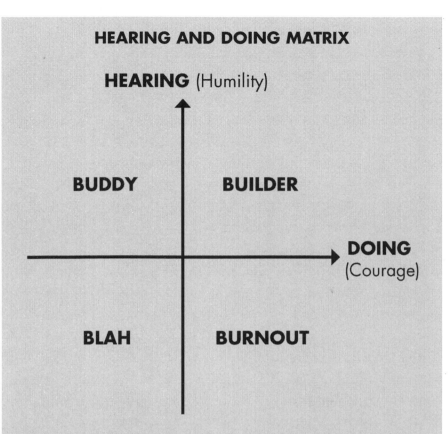

HEARING AND DOING MATRIX

HEARING (Humility)

BUDDY **BUILDER**

DOING (Courage)

BLAH **BURNOUT**

BURNOUT: When we are the foolish builder, we are not hearing. Instead we are all doing. We are constantly striving and not ever seeking wisdom from God. We all have different seasons when we have our head down in the busyness of life and never come up for air. This is not sustainable and leads to burnout.

BLAH: If you are not hearing or doing, then life is just blah. If you are reading this book, you are not in this category.

BUDDY: We can find ourselves in a season of all hearing and no doing. We are hearing what God says, but we don't have the courage to act. We may be going to church and hearing great messages, listening to spiritual podcasts, but we are not putting this knowledge into action. We become a buddy and do not speak truth into people's lives or take bold steps in our own life. We are in a season of playing it safe.

BUILDER: Jesus calls us to be builders. He wants us to have the humility to hear His word and then have the courage to act. We need to be building into others, building businesses, and building our own lives.

hear God. *Doing* is the courage to take action.

I have secular clients with whom I cannot talk specifically about God. Interestingly, however, even people who don't believe in God see solitude as valuable, as a game changer. Terms like *mindfulness* and *self-care* are popular these days. My secular clients talk about how critical those quiet times are. They talk about the life-transforming power of yoga, meditation, cycling, running, or some other activity that gets them out of their busyness. All of these activities are an effort, I think, to slow down and connect with a greater power. I call this greater power God.

GROWING IN SPIRITUAL CAPITAL

How can you grow in your spiritual capital this week? Can you spend more time in prayer? Can you journal this week? What Scripture are you reading?

We need to increase our time in solitude so that we can hear from God. But solitude needs to be intentional and structured. Unstructured solitude can lead to our thoughts drifting into thinking about our work to-do list or deceiving us by thinking of only fears and doubts. However, if we structure our journaling with questions and Scripture, it can lead to clarity and confidence.

Another worthwhile exercise is to plot yourself on the Hearing and Doing Matrix.

- Where are you on a macro level? Overall, in which category would you say you spend the most time?

- Now identify a few areas where you are in the Burnout category—doing all the work, all the striving, but you need to ask God for insight.

- What about the Buddy category? In what areas are you hearing from God but not taking action?

- What about the Builder quadrant? These are spots in your life where you are being obedient to God, doing what he says. Well done!

Why is this important? Growing our spiritual capital is about prioritizing hearing from God and following in obedience. The more we invest in spiritual capital, the better we will be in tune with God's voice to know when He is speaking to us. The more we obey His voice, we grow in confidence and boldness to continue to follow His direction.

However, when we don't grow our spiritual capital, we run the risk of hearing only from our peers and other like-minded folks. We also become timid, afraid to take bold, God-directed steps. Without direction from God, we could go down the path of self-destruction.

5

RELATIONAL CAPITAL

Who Is Investing in You, and Who Are You Investing In?

A few years ago, I realized I had zero friends. I know that sounds extreme, but being honest, at that time in my life I had nobody I was doing life with.

Yes, I had a lot of guys I could call and meet up for coffee or beer, but I did not have a group of guys who knew me other than on a surface level. I could talk sports, weather, and other superficial topics with guys, but nobody at that time truly knew what I was processing in my relationship with God, my wife, my kids, and the deeper areas of life.

I had been in a season when I was focused on work and home, not my deeper self. I had started a new job as president of sales for a national contractor, so every week I was traveling to different parts of the country, meeting with our leadership team, sales personnel, key clients and partners, as well as various projects to see the operations team at work.

When it came to my family, I felt bad I was gone all week, so on the weekends I was all-in with date nights, playing with the kids, and doing house projects. Then Monday would come around, and I would start the rotation again.

I felt empty. I was busy and doing well at work, my home life was good, but I felt almost robotic. I was going from place to place but not having a lot to give. Without friends pouring into me, my own cup was empty, and I was unable to pour into others.

We all get into seasons of life when we are giving to our work and our family but lose sight of community. Do any of the following statements resonate with you?

- You are coming out of infant season with your newborn and feeling the need to reach out to friends.

- You just got done with a busy soccer or dance season with your kids and have some free time for more of a social life.

- Maybe you're traveling a lot for work lately and not able to connect with your friends.

- As you pause to assess your conversations with friends, you realize they are superficial, and you need to go deeper.

- You have gotten in a rut of coming home from work, then sitting on the coach and watching TV.

In order for us to thrive at work and home, we need to be pouring into friends and have them pour into us. A key benefit of spending time with friends is that you realize you are not alone. The stresses you are experiencing in your marriage, the challenges with your kids, and the difficult boss or coworkers at work—they are all normal.

One factor that contributed to my having an affair about fifteen years ago is I did not have guys in my life with whom I was having conversations of depth. We were talking about sports, weather, stocks, and all the other surface-level conversations. In my naivety I assumed everybody else's marriage was perfect and I was the only one having issues. We had stresses of Holly and me both working, schedule demands, work travels, trying to balance "our" time versus "friend" time. I kept thinking something was wrong with me and my marriage, but the reality is that the challenges we were facing were normal. I just didn't talk about depths of marriage with friends, so I didn't know others were experiencing the same difficulties.

WHAT IS RELATIONAL CAPITAL?

If we are not careful and the only people in our lives are coworkers and family, we will drift into isolation. We will not have friends to do adventures with, we will not have people to talk to in times of stress, friends to hold us accountable, or friends to celebrate the victories with.

We were not designed to be alone. Just because you are with coworkers, or even with your family, does not mean you are in community with others. You need to have adults, in addition to your spouse, who really know you and you know them.

So often in today's culture we are expected to be independent. For men it's "pull yourself up by your own bootstraps" and "be a man." For women it's "stand strong" and "don't show weakness" in the workplace. All of these messages are screaming for independence and not community.

Yet what happens to the lone wolf? He gets taken out. The same thing happens to humans. When you try to do life alone, you get taken out by Satan. You have doubt, insecurities, and pride, and you may even create an imposter-self. We were designed for community, not only with God but with others.

Jesus modeled this. He had a few different orbits of people in His life. We know the stories about His work among the masses, like feeding five thousand people or turning water into wine at a wedding. But we may overlook how intentional He was when He was not doing miracles. Jesus often spent time with His twelve disciples, and within that group Jesus had three He spent the most time with—Peter, John, and James. Jesus knew that for His work to be sustainable, in addition to His time with the Father and solitude, He needed community.

I just saw this quote the other day: "Nobody ever talks about Jesus's greatest miracle: that Jesus had twelve close friends in His thirties." How true is that?! We have great friends in our high school years and usually get a new group of friends in college, maybe our closest friends. Then when we get into the work world, our number of friends starts to decrease as we focus on our careers. Friendships further decline as people have families and more work responsibility. By the time we're in our thirties and forties, many of us have very few, if any, close friends.

In Mark 6:30–33, after Jesus had been performing miracles and giving numerous teachings, He knew it was time to get away and spend time with His buddies. In verse 31 Jesus says, "Come away by yourselves to a desolate place and rest a while." Jesus knew He and His disciples needed to just hang out together.

In Luke 10, when Jesus sent out seventy-two people to go before Him into the towns and villages to spread the gospel, He sent them out two by two. He knew that living a life of intentionality could not be done alone. He knew that if He sent out these people by themselves, they would get discouraged over time and eventually quit.

GROWING IN RELATIONAL CAPITAL

Consider some questions:

- Who are you doing life with?

- Who is your inner circle?

- How can you grow in relational capital over the next few weeks?

- Do you need to be intentional with any family members and work on building trust?

- Do you need to grab a coffee or beer with a friend you have not seen in a while?

Once you have reached out to some friends, I encourage you to go for deeper conversations. Don't just talk weather and sports. Instead, look to have conversations of depth. Yes, deep conversations can get messy, but they also lead to greater impact in each other's life.

List the closest friends in your life and reach out to them!

6

PHYSICAL CAPITAL

Are You Controlling Your Schedule, or Does It Control You?

One day I was opening the mail at home and got a letter from the gym where I'm a member. Unfortunately, I hadn't been there for a little while, so I was curious what the letter was about. It was a kick in the pants. I was already beating myself up for not working out lately and feeling sluggish. Then I read the letter, which said in effect, "We have not seen you in a while," and went on to list all the benefits of the gym so I wouldn't quit altogether.

It made me mad to get the letter, but it was the wake-up call I needed. I was making excuses for why I couldn't work out. I had to stay up late to get work done, needed to get to the office early in the morning, had to meet this person for drinks to network. The excuses went on for weeks.

I was putting other activities in front of working out. For me to be at my best, though, I need to work out three to four times a week. When I take care of my physical capital, I have more to give. When I am eating right and working out, I have more energy, I am more self-confident, and I can handle stress better. When I don't work out, I feel sluggish and give in to the temptation of unhealthy food, which leads to my being more irritable.

WHAT IS PHYSICAL CAPITAL?

Physical capital is about optimizing our time and energy so that we have more to give others in our work and home. We do this by managing our calendar and body by going to the gym, getting rest, having solitude, being intentional with our commute, and other practices related to energy management.

In order to provide a return on God's investment, ourselves, we need to have the time and energy to do so. We need to view life as a marathon, not a sprint.

Physical capital is about managing your schedule, so it does not manage you. It's also about managing your body so that you have energy to invest in others. When you are out of shape, tired, having a sugar crash, or when anything is zapping your energy, you can't pour into others.

SLOW DOWN

One area where I continue to improve in my life and encourage clients to do the same is to find more rest. Not necessarily napping, although that is not a bad thing, just downtime. Time to slow down; time to think; time to be still.

Unfortunately, finding rest in our culture is considered a sign of weakness. Whenever you ask anybody how they have been lately, they say "busy." We say it as a badge of honor, because if we are not busy, we must not be successful.

We never say no to things because we don't want to let people down or feel inadequate in our ability to get things done. We are allowing our schedule to control us, instead of us controlling our schedule. As client and friend Chris Caddell, chairman of Heritage Bank, says, "The quantity of our no's will drive the quality of our yes's."

When I am intentional with physical capital, I look to find more moments of rest. I ask myself, "Do I need to make that conference call or attend that meeting, or would I be better off using that time for solitude?"

FRUITFUL AND FULFILLING

Consider this question when evaluating a rest activity: Does this truly provide rest, or is it another source of noise and stress? If I watch a sporting event by myself and my team losses, for example, it is not restful. As a matter of fact, it causes more stress because I think I wasted two to three hours watching the game and wasn't productive. However, being an extrovert, if I watch that same game with a friend, it is very restful regardless of who wins or loses because I am having a conversation with a friend. On the other hand, my wife, who's an introvert, really enjoys watching TV and finds rest during that time alone.

Years ago, when I lived in Kansas City, I listened to sports radio every day while I drove around making sales calls thinking I was resting in between work activities. I found myself getting frustrated with decisions the sports teams were making or the politics involved with the stadium relocation or you name it.

Over time I stopped listening to sports radio, the news, and NPR because I found them to be more stressful than fruitful. Occasionally I may listen to them, but now when I am in the car, I am more likely to have the radio off. I tend to use my commuting time to be thankful for the day so far or praying and prepping for the meetings that are coming up.

Here's another helpful question to consider: Is this activity fruitful for the Kingdom and fulfilling to my heart?

"Fruitful for the Kingdom" means it serves God's purposes and no one is negatively impacted by it, such as spending time with good friends or family, reading, or watching a movie that brings you closer to His character. Examples of activities that are not fruitful for the Kingdom include looking at porn, gambling, or other activities that negatively impact others.

"Fulfilling to the heart" means the activity is a blessing to your soul. It fills you up. For me that means no to sports on TV by myself or playing video games and yes to being with others or working on a blog post or new content to inspire others.

FRUITFULNESS VS. ABIDING

In John 15, Jesus teaches a parable about the various stages of life of a vine, ranging from healthy and bearing fruit to being pruned if not bearing enough fruit or none at all.

The Work vs. Rest Pendulum is a tool that shows this continuum between work and rest. Work and areas of fruitfulness are at one end of the pendulum, and the area where we are resting and abiding is the other. The following are the four stages:

- **WORK/FRUITFULNESS:** fruit is growing in this area and we need to continue to cultivate

- **GROWING:** an area where investment needs to continue because it is developing into something greater

- **PRUNING:** removing activities or tasks that are not bearing fruit anymore

- **REST/ABIDE:** reflection, naps, solitude, and connection with God

WORK VS. REST PENDULUM

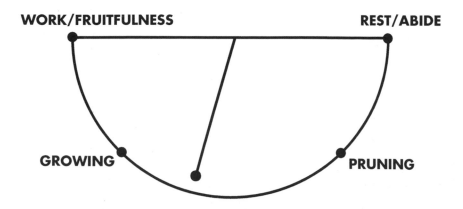

When it comes to work and rest, we can count on Newton's third law: For every action, there is an equal and opposite reaction. Where we are bearing fruit and having success, we need the counterbalance of rest and abiding with God. For example, we need to counterbalance the high output we give toward execution, delivery, and performance with the equal and opposite reaction of developing ideas, strategizing, reflecting, and solitude.

The Bible says God created humans on the sixth day. On the seventh day God said to rest, calling it the Sabbath. See that?! Our first day on earth was dedicated to rest! God created us to rest and then go to work.

We are to work from a position of rest, not rest from work. When we are working after rest, we are going into work with full hearts and energy. Full of ideas and desire to be productive and effective. When we are always using the weekend to recover, then when Monday rolls around, we dread it. We are limping back into work for another week of hammering things out.

STRIVING VS. CRASHING

We all find ourselves in seasons where we push the limits of work vs. rest, and it becomes striving vs. crashing. We strive so hard at work, going to and from kids' activities, and participating in social engagements that we end up crashing at night and on the weekends. The reality is that we can only go so hard until our body and mind can't go any more.

A successful professional once told me she was convinced that striving and crashing was the only way to win. This individual was meeting deadlines, getting incredible new job opportunities, getting kids to and from practice, and so she felt like she was being successful. She admitted that crashing was the only way since she had young kids and both she and her husband had demanding jobs. She said they would just recalibrate when the kids were older.

Striving vs. crashing may feel like it is working for a season, but it is not sustainable. Yes, we need to do it at times because a big deadline is approaching or the end of the quarter is near. But to be a great leader at work and home, we need to recalibrate sooner rather than later.

Striving and crashing is not sustainable because we create bad habits such as addictions or coping mechanisms to keep it afloat: binge TV watching, aimless social media, alcohol, porn, etc. These bad habits are difficult to break even when the deadline is over!

SELF-DIAGNOSIS

The following list will help you determine if you are currently in a season of striving and crashing.

- You have zero capacity. If there are any big changes in your life that require more of your time, you will cave because nothing can give. You have a fender bender, an employee leaves, a kid breaks an arm—you have no capacity to handle an extra load like one of these. The "straw that broke the camel's back" applies here.

- You are not spending time in reflection. This may not seem like a big deal to you, but many sources, including the book *Lead Yourself First*, state solitude is critical to leaders because it brings self-awareness and emotional balance.

- You are not present with the people around you. Your mind is on other things—your next meeting, your next conversation. But you are not present with those in the room. Most often your spouse or kids are the victims of this one.

- You are emotionally unstable. You are quick to snap at others, maybe even family members. You beat yourself up for minor errors at work. You are hard on yourself and others.

- You are not dependent on God. You are dependent on yourself. You think you need to work around the clock to get the job done. You think if you don't reply to that one last email, make that phone call, the whole thing will come crumbling down. (No, it won't, by the way.)

Unfortunately, the illusion of striving and crashing is that it is working, and for a time you look like everyone else who is also running around like crazy. But mark my words: striving and crashing is a ticking time bomb.

GROWING IN PHYSICAL CAPITAL

Consider these questions:

- How will you improve your physical capital this week?

- Do you need to go for a run or exercise this week?

- Do you need to watch less TV and focus on a few other things instead that will give you fruit?

- Do you need to say no to a few meetings or activities this week?

- How do you need to change your food intake this week? Quality and quantity?

- Do you need to go to bed earlier and/or wake up earlier?

Physical capital is interesting because it shows immediate gains or losses. We all have experienced a week we feel great, only to have an unhealthy week of travel and fast food the next week. When we don't feel good physically, it affects our work. We are sluggish, not as creative, even moody. On the other hand, when we are feeling good physically, we are more confident, have energy to give to others, and are quick to take action.

Knowing how it can change from week to week validates how a small improvement in this capital can make a big difference. Physical capital is the great equalizer, as we all have twenty-four hours in a day, yet we can range from bad days to great days, so this capital must be taken seriously.

7

INTELLECTUAL CAPITAL

How Are You Growing in Knowledge?

Every once in a while, maybe a couple times a year, I go through a funk where I am bored or depressed. My self-talk is not that great. I can't psyche myself up. I feel I have nothing to give my clients. I almost feel as though I will be exposed. A fraud. Not competent.

I find myself using the same Scriptures with clients because I am not hearing anything new from God. Using the same quotes, stories, and pieces of content I always do. As if the well is running dry.

Over time I have learned that when I am not intentional about spending time with God or investing in learning from others, I start to feel defeated. When I am intentional about what I put into my brain, I rejuvenate myself and feel invigorated because I want to share what I am learning.

WHAT IS INTELLECTUAL CAPITAL?

Intellectual capital is about insight and ideas. This capital is about the creativity and knowledge we are able to invest in others. It's about staying healthy mentally. Leaders are learners, so the wise are always humble and hungry to learn more.

This capital is also cumulative when we use it to teach others. As we gain more experience and knowledge and regularly share, then more ideas and insights will emerge. We need to be growing in intellectual capital so that we have applicable information to teach others as needed in their life, whether personally or professionally.

JESUS AS THE EXAMPLE

Similar to the other capitals, Jesus modeled this one as well. Jesus was not a slacker in His intellectual capital. Yes, Jesus cast out demons and healed people, but He is most known for being the best teacher who ever lived.

Jesus was always teaching in metaphors, illustrations, and parables to the amazement of the crowds. At the end of the Sermon on the Mount, Matthew 7:28–29 says, "And when Jesus finished these sayings, the crowds were astonished at his teaching, for he was teaching them as one who had authority, and not as their scribes."

Jesus's intelligence was also modeled through His leadership and discipleship. Great leaders teach others to become great leaders as well. The many lessons that Jesus taught to the masses, He was intentional to share with His disciples—teaching them to be current and relevant with their audiences as well as great storytellers to engage their audiences.

We see this multiplication model in Acts 4 when Peter and

John spoke to the rulers, elders, and high priests in Jerusalem about why they continued to preach about Jesus, even after His death. After Peter and John defended their reason for teaching the crowds, the audience was amazed. It says in Acts 4:13, "Now when they saw the boldness of Peter and John, and perceived that they were uneducated, common men, they were astonished. And they recognized that they had been with Jesus."

Yes, some people are born with an intelligence advantage, but through learning from others, we all can grow in our intellectual capital, just like Peter and John did by spending time with Jesus.

LEARNING TAKES INTENTIONALITY

We have all been around the individual who can provide the applicable nugget to share based on the conversation taking place. The right inspirational quote at just the right time. The new marketing strategy to apply to the business. The new way to communicate your brand identity. A movie or book story that is helpful. These people were not born with this knowledge. They learn it by putting in the time.

Leaders make time to read books for inspiration and listen to podcasts to sharpen their skills. These individuals also learn from others face to face. They hire coaches for a season, meet with mentors consistently, and surround themselves with thought leaders.

However, it takes intentionality. When we get busy, we tend to get discouraged during our free time and just zone out and watch Netflix. On our commute we stick to Top 40 music and just go brain dead during our drive. We don't meet with coaches or mentors because we think, "I got this," or "I don't need help."

THE INTELLECTUAL CAPITAL LEADER IN MY LIFE

Tom always seemed to be just a step ahead of the rest of us with a new idea. No doubt he was smart, but time after time, his intelligence was proved by intentional learning at the time, plus teaching others along the way.

In a rebranding meeting with a consultant, he contributed very relevant ideas. Eventually, the consultant asked if he had ever done a rebranding. Come to find out, he had recently been reading marketing books in preparation for the rebranding.

Tom and I were pursuing a partnership with a competitor and he sent me blogs, articles, and videos on partnering strategy, negotiation tactics, and market and product fit. Not only was he sharing them with me, he was reading and watching them himself, even though he had done numerous partnerships in the past. He wanted to make sure we both were sharpening our skills on these topics.

Tom was also the first leader that I saw hand out books like candy. He had influential books in his office credenza and would hand them out to people as he felt prompted.

Individuals with high intellectual capital tend to be great storytellers, not because of an innate ability, although some may have a unique gift, but mostly due to learning from the quantity of stories they have heard. It could be a story from a movie, podcast, mentor, or book that they share at a meeting. Tom was always able to share an inspirational story about an individual or a company that was applicable to the topic in the room.

I am also grateful to Tom because he was the one who encouraged me to get an executive coach. Although we worked well together, he knew the value he received in his career from coaches, and he knew I would benefit from the outside perspective as well.

BE CAREFUL

Motive is very important for this capital. When we invest in our intellectual capital, we need to make sure we're doing it for the right reason—to nurture a healthy mindset. A pitfall I have to make a conscious effort to avoid is trying to increase in my intellectual capital so I can be "the man" and provide all the answers. When that happens, I know I need to refocus on learning and staying current so that I can help meet clients where they're at, not so they think I am the smartest in the room. I want to be able to point clients to the right book or podcast to supplement their learning.

GROWING IN INTELLECTUAL CAPITAL

Consider these questions:

- How are you growing in your intellectual capital?

- What books are you reading?

- What podcasts are you listening to?

- What are you curious to learn more about?

- Is this a season you need to grow intellectually in your job because you are in a new role?

- How can you grow in your intellectual capital over the next season? Next sixty days?

- Is it time you hire a coach?

An important note here: We need to be growing in both spiritual and intellectual capital, not just one or the other. We need first to go to God, as mentioned in the spiritual capital section, but it's also important to grow in our intellectual capital so we can stay relevant and current with the latest thinking.

8

FINANCIAL CAPITAL

Do You Have a Scarcity or Abundance Mindset?

A few years ago, I was sitting in a chair next to my wife in a place you never want to be—a bankruptcy attorney's office. When you exchange vows with your bride and say, "for richer or poorer," you don't really think about being "poorer." At least, I didn't. I assumed I'd be successful, provide for my family, and we would be richer, not poorer!

But on this particular day we were definitely poorer. We had hit rock bottom.

Before the recession in 2008, I was looking to make additional money outside my full-time sales job. So I decided to invest in real estate. I even had thoughts of being the next big real estate tycoon.

The first house my wife and I bought was purchased via a foreclosure, and in four weeks we had it market ready and sold for a profit of $17,000. It was incredible! We were well on our way, or so we thought.

I then put together a package of five homes, some purchased with partners, some without, and we met with a bank. This was before the recession, so it was way too easy to purchase real estate (one reason the recession happened in the first place). We purchased all these houses with the intent to remodel and then sell them. It was the "buy and flip" concept. But during our construction and rehab process of these homes, the recession hit and changed our investment into an enormous headache.

Instead of flipping them, we had to rent them. Unfortunately, at that time our area had a surplus of houses due to investors facing the same dilemma, so the price of rent also fell. We were able to rent the five houses, but they were all lower than rent value before the recession.

Every month we had negative cash flow, plus we had to pay for repairs along the way, plus the expense of new carpet and paint when renters changed. We did all we could to keep the houses afloat.

We could have abandoned the houses like some landlords did during the early years of the recession, but we didn't feel right about it. We depleted our savings and maxed out our credit cards, but eventually we ran out of time and money. Finally, we were able to sell the houses but below market value in a sale, a short sale, and even foreclosure. Holly and I didn't know how, and if, we would ever climb out of our real estate deficit. We had creditors calling us, large credit card debts, and an awful credit score.

So on this particular day we were sitting in the chairs of a bankruptcy attorney to explore a possible exit strategy. As the attorney laid out our options, it seemed like the easy way out would be to pay the $4,000 or so to the attorney, file for bankruptcy, and start over.

But while we were there, I felt God tell me we didn't have to do this. There was another way.

Even though I didn't know at all how there could be another way, I was open-minded to the idea. I even had a peace about it. After years of stress and wishing for a way out, finally within inches of the solution, I actually had a peace about exploring God's other way.

As I continued to sit there listening to the attorney, I felt God say, *"I will get you out of this. There is another way."* So at that moment I said we were ready to go. As I nudged my wife to leave, I could tell she felt the same peace.

We left the bankruptcy attorney and began the long climb out of the valley. We made it out without having to file for bankruptcy, but if I'm honest, I do have some mental scars from it.

DON'T WAIT FOR ROCK BOTTOM

Our finances are most often a private matter, so we mask our relationship to money until it is too late. We may undervalue money and allow it to control us. We have bad spending habits, live above our means, and build up credit card debt. On the other hand, we may overvalue money and turn it into a god. When money is our definition of success, we strive for the next promotion, even at the expense of other capitals.

However, when we hit rock bottom, the truth is often exposed on how we view money. The debt we owe. The greed of wanting more. The broken relationships of never being home. The fear and anxiety of never enough. The amount of stuff we own in storage.

WHAT IS FINANCIAL CAPITAL?

Financial capital is the last of the five capitals because

although we need it as a resource, we can't let it control our thinking.

We all know money can't buy happiness. We may feel like it does temporarily, but then the new car smell wears off. The new house needs paint. The new clothes start to fade.

Many of us get tripped up with money. God knew this would be a problem, which is why He said you cannot love both God and money (Matthew 6:24).

Financial capital is about the money we have to invest in ourselves and others. Money is to be a resource, not an idol.

OUR AGREEMENTS WITH MONEY

Events in our life shape our perception of money and how we interact with it. Below are some examples you may relate to:

- The incredible feeling of wealth and success as you bought clothes and furniture using your credit card, yet the feeling of poverty and defeat when you saw the credit card bill and knew you couldn't afford it.

- The feeling of accomplishment when you got the raise or bonus and were excited to get ahead in your finances, only to be living paycheck to paycheck in six months.

- You have always been surrounded with a wealthy lifestyle from childhood to present day. Your wealth—as reflected in your car, your country club membership, your house, and other luxuries—has a way of defining who you are.

- Or you may have childhood memories of living in poverty and you still feel you can't get ahead financially. You feel like it is "just not in the cards" for you to have wealth.

Our life experiences lead to "agreements" we have with money, beliefs that drive our actions and mindset toward money.

QUESTIONING OUR AGREEMENTS

On my bad days I have a scarcity mindset. My self-talk is that I was not meant for abundance. I have to do all the work on my own because God is not looking out for me. In those times I see this scarcity mindset play out in even small ways, such as getting alligator arms and being slow to grab the bill in a group setting.

This mindset causes me to begin to strive and assign "making money" as my top priority. I start to believe I am the provider for my family because God does not care. When money is my top priority, it consumes my mind, distances me from God, and adds stress in my life. I think back to being in the bankruptcy chair and allow that experience to define me. A failure. Not a provider for my family.

On my good days, however, I remember the rest of that story. I think about how God got me out of that chair and provided a path for Holly and me to recover financially. I know I need to steward money well; however, God is the ultimate provider—by opening doors, providing connections, and so much more. I am able to release the financial stress and put my faith in God.

GROWING IN FINANCIAL CAPITAL

Whatever our relationship with money is, we can begin to shift our mindset today. Don't wait. By questioning where your spending is going and the "why" behind the spending, you will be able to dissect your money relationship. Maybe you are a saver because you fear not having enough money someday. On the other hand, you may be a spender looking for happiness today.

CONSIDER THESE QUESTIONS:

- Where in your life do you have a scarcity mindset?

- Where can you get more intentional in your finances so you reduce your stress level?

- What are areas where you need to steward your money better?

- How can you remind yourself everything belongs to God?

- Who is the wise counsel in your life giving you advice on money management?

- How can you be more generous with your money?

It is difficult to see quick wins in financial capital due to the time it can take to pay off a credit card debt or build a nest egg. Don't let the long game discourage you from beginning, because if you don't start today, then tomorrow is one day less toward your financial goals. As my wealth manager illustrates, if you have high cholesterol and go see your doctor, you still have high cholesterol. However, the doctor can begin to help you lower your cholesterol. Same thing with financial capital. Your financial status is what it is. However, starting to move toward a more generous mindset and better stewardship of your money can start now.

We need to review our relationship with money and engage with professionals in this industry to better understand ways to improve.

9

UP AND TO THE RIGHT

How to Handle Setbacks

Great leaders are self-aware, and the value of the five capitals tool is it brings awareness to your current mindset when used as a filter. When I am out of sorts or stressed about finances or feeling fat and sluggish or whatever, I use this tool to recalibrate. The value of the five capitals is it helps you to evaluate yourself and make sure your priorities are in the right order.

Now it is your turn to assess yourself! Go to www.winathomefirstbook.com/resources to see how you rank!

UP AND TO THE RIGHT

It's like clockwork. About every third or fourth call with a client we have a setback. We have a few calls in a row that are great. We're seeing breakthroughs and making progress. Then the setback happens.

On good calls the client is high energy and usually comes excited to share and give updates—how they went on a date with their spouse, how they worked out, what they heard from God, the great conversation with a direct report, the new customer account. Then for one of our calls they don't come with positive energy. They do not have a list made out. They most often didn't do the action items from our last conversation.

We all feel that way occasionally. Maybe we played too hard that weekend and we're tired. The project we are working on is frustrating because it is not coming together. The task we delegated to an employee is not getting done to our liking. Our quiet time has been nonexistent, so we haven't heard from God. We all get discouraged from time to time.

When these low-energy calls happen, I remind the client we are making progress, and I share the idea of "up and to the right."

Graphs that show growth go up and to the right. As you move further across the X axis, you want the Y axis to be increasing.

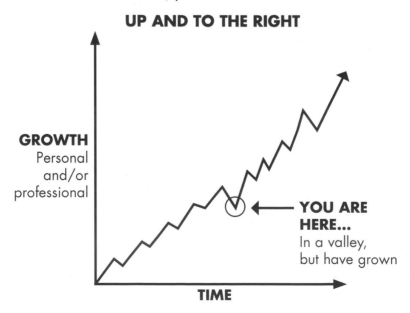

UP AND TO THE RIGHT

GROWTH
Personal
and/or
professional

YOU ARE HERE...
In a valley,
but have grown

TIME

But it's very seldom a straight line. There are peaks and valleys. Today may not seem as good as yesterday, but as you look at the trend, the line is going up.

When we are growing in life, this is normal. You are not alone when you hit the valley. Often, we create positive habits over the course of a few weeks, then we miss a day or two, so the graph dips. Then we can get back on track and continue the upward trend.

What I love about people who are growing is that they get so passionate about their new self, they forget about their old self. Sometimes clients will get discouraged because they have not journaled for a few days. I have to remind them that before we were working together in a coach/client relationship, not only were they not journaling on a regular basis, they didn't even own a journal!

The principle of "up and to the right" is about looking over your shoulder and seeing your progress. Yes, today may be a setback, or this week, or maybe it has been a rough month. But look how far you have come! Your new habit today was not even on your radar a few months ago.

This "new you" was aspirational, and now it is actual.

You never thought you could exercise and lose that ten pounds. You thought the relationship with your family member was lost, and although it is not perfect, you guys are talking again. You never viewed yourself as an entrepreneur, yet now you are making money doing something you love.

TIME TO RECALIBRATE

As the Bible story goes in Matthew 14:22–32, Peter started to walk on water, then he took his eyes off Jesus, lost a little bit of faith, and started to sink. We do the same thing. We build up enough confidence, courage, maybe even a little insanity, and go for it.

We get out of the boat. We take the risk. Then we get nervous, forget about our dreams and passions, and instead think of the risks and naysayers, so we start to sink.

The secret of great leaders is they are quick to recalibrate. When they see a dip, they believe it's temporary, that the overall trend line is up and to the right. They quickly make an adjustment to stop the negative movement and get back on track.

If you are in a valley, it's time to recalibrate. We all get in the valley from time to time. No need to hit the panic or eject button. Look over your shoulder and see all the good that has happened in your life to this point. Your life is a small story that is part of a much greater story God is writing. By looking over your shoulder, you can see how God has been building into you. Your education. Your family. Your community. What you thought you couldn't do, you did—not on your own accord, but through God's provision. You have great friendships, and yes, you need to steward them well, but it is by God's provision they are in your life. You may have great business acumen, but it is by God's provision you have the job you do. Your business may be profitable, and you have stewarded it well, but this too has been by God's provision.

Looking over our shoulder allows us to see what God has built in our lives. We then can move forward in confidence and take action, knowing God will provide for us in the future just like He has in the past.

Where do you want to go? What are you praying for God to build in your future?

PRIDE AND PESSIMISM

Jesus knew peaks and valleys would be hard for us, just as it was in His time, because it takes us further away from Him. In Luke 3:5 Jesus quotes from the prophet Isaiah, saying, "Every valley shall be filled, and every mountain and hill shall be made low." He was speaking to the Pharisees about their pride at the mountain top, as well as the valley for those feeling distant due to their sins. Jesus came to level the road. Why is that important? Peaks have a way of leading us to pride and self-dependence, whereas valleys bring pessimism and self-doubt.

When life is going great, instead of turning it into a peak of pride, thinking we are doing this all on our own, we need to remain humble and dependent on God, knowing His provision and protection is how we got to this peak. On the flipside, when we hit the valley, instead of getting down and depressed, we need to lean on God knowing He has gotten us out of every valley in our lives before now, and He will again!

In the areas of your life that are currently peaks, make sure to thank God. Through gratitude we remain humble. In the valley areas of your life, make sure to pull God in. Thank Him for getting you out of valleys in the past and ask for His help now!

10

HOW ARE YOU TEMPTED?

Understanding Our Three Major Temptations

A few months ago, I attended a conference in Phoenix and was so inspired. The talks, the videos, the role-playing activities, everything. I wrote down notes from the speakers as well as random thoughts on how I was going to implement these ideas when I got home. I even purchased a book from one of the speakers and was excited to read it!

When I got back home, the book went on my shelf and the notes in a folder. Yes, I still plan to get to them, but due to the demands of work and new inspirations, they are quickly becoming distant.

I love the term "seminar land" because it captures the reality so many of us have experienced. We get inspired but struggle to implement due to external demands and internal fears. We go home, get sucked back into work and home life, and don't make any significant changes. We remain at status quo. Same person we were before the conference. All inspiration, zero transformation.

I do not want that to happen with you and the inspiration you receive from this book. My goal and prayer for this book is that it begins a transformation in your life. A big part of making sure this happens is becoming aware of the obstacles that get in the way of our moving forward. If we're aware of them, we can overcome them as opposed to being surprised and getting knocked backwards.

Nik Kinley, author of *Talent Intelligence*, said Americans spend $2–$4 billion a year on personality tests, trying to better ourselves. We are all trying to leverage our strengths, our personality, our emotional intelligence, and our leadership potential. I too have participated in these tests and enjoy seeing the results. As a matter of fact, thanks to the inspirational conference in Phoenix just mentioned, I am certified to do DISC training.

I'm a fan of these tests, but they are limited. Yes, they tell us our strengths and weaknesses, but they also assume we are in a good place mentally. What happens when we are feeling lonely? Insecure? Not good enough? Concerned we don't have enough in the bank account for our kids' college? Worrying about whether we will get the next promotion? Concerned about whether the new project team likes us and our contributions?

It's important to understand our strengths, but not at the expense of knowing our temptations and our places of weakness. We can't truly live into our strengths if we continually get tripped up over internal shortcomings and blind spots.

TEMPTATIONS

We know the phrase: our greatest strength can become our weakness. For me, it is approval of others. I love connecting with people, talking with people in the neighborhood, getting to know coworkers in the office. I'm an extrovert and evangelist. Throughout my life I have found myself in various roles such as "king" of the high school dance and later "king" of the engineering school in college. Leader of different teams. Social chair in many groups. Recruiter for organizations.

However, my strength connecting with people and winning their approval has a dark side. Whether or not people approve of me can start to dominate my thoughts. Do they like me? Am I the best coach they have ever had? Am I the best husband? The best dad? Why was I not included in that work decision; do they not value my input?

I want to be in the room where everybody is; otherwise I feel left out. FOMO—fear of missing out. I am often last to leave the party, afraid I will miss something.

Even as I write this, I am in Montana helping lead a New Frontier retreat for men, and I am battling with approval. While I am here, I teach a few of the sessions, but at other times my mind can start to drift, and I wonder what the guys think of me. Do they like me? Are they laughing at my jokes? Do they believe me? Am I doing a good job? Are their hearts moving due to my teaching? Are they disappointed I am teaching and not Chris, the founder of The New Frontier?

This is an ongoing struggle for me, but a teaching about when Jesus was tempted in the desert has been very helpful.

THREE TEMPTATIONS

After Jesus was baptized by John and affirmed by God, the Holy Spirit leads Jesus out into the wilderness for forty days. Jesus fasts in the desert, so he is hungry, hot, tired, and lonely. How Jesus overcomes these temptations, especially while in His weakened state, is a guide for us.

Appetite

In Luke 4:3–4, the devil says to Jesus, "If you are the Son of God, command this stone to become bread." And Jesus answers him, "It is written, 'Man shall not live by bread alone,'" a quote from the Old Testament book of Deuteronomy.

This testing represents *appetite*. Always wanting more. More food, more booze, more cars, more clothes. This temptation is where you find yourself consuming things to make you feel better about yourself. With this temptation there is a void in your heart that only Jesus can fill, but you use temporal things to try to fill it.

In times of stress and self-defeat, do you tend to overeat? Overdrink? When you are lonely, do you binge watch TV? When you feel defeated, does "retail therapy" help you feel better about yourself? Is there an Amazon box on your front porch most days?

Ambition

Next, in Luke 4:5–8, the devil takes Jesus up to the hilltop and shows him all the kingdoms of the world. He says, "To you I will give all this authority and their glory, for it has been delivered to me, and I give it to whom I will. If you, then, will worship me, it will all be yours." Once again Jesus responds with God's words from Deuteronomy: "It is written, 'You shall worship the Lord your God, and him only shall you serve.'"

This testing represents *ambition*. Striving hard to get the right job title. To get the corner office. Constantly worrying about whether you are doing the right things to get to the top. An endless battle of comparing your career to somebody else's. Comparing someone else's successful life to your ordinary life. Comparing someone's "FakeBook" life to your "blooper reel."

In times of stress and self-defeat, do you work late to make sure your career is progressing? Instead of spending time with your family, are you always working on the weekends? Are you constantly comparing the speed of your career growth to that of others?

Approval

The third and last temptation in Luke 4:9–13 is when the devil takes Jesus to Jerusalem and sets Him on the pinnacle of the temple. "If you are the Son of God," the devil says to Jesus, "throw yourself down from here, for it is written, 'He will command his angels concerning you, to guard you,' and 'On their hands will they bear you up.'" Jesus responds, again quoting Scripture in Deuteronomy, "It is said, 'You shall not put the Lord your God to the test.'"

This testing represents *approval*. The idea that we get our self-worth and value from others. Constantly wondering what people think of us. Doing things or saying yes to invitations because we want people to like us.

In times of isolation and self-defeat, do you look to others for validation by laughing at your jokes? Do you send out unnecessary text messages to get a response? Do you ask questions about your performance or contribution at the last meeting? Do you volunteer too much at nonprofits, social gatherings, or your kids' school so people will like you?

HOW ARE YOU TEMPTED?

As you pursue your dreams and goals, you need to know how the devil tempts you. You have to be on guard for what your weak spots are. We can fall victim to any of these three temptations, and at different times in our lives one could be more prominent than the others, but typically one of the temptations is primary and another is secondary.

My primary temptation is approval. I want to be the most liked person on the project team. I want to be the favorite neighbor. I want to be everybody's friend. If I am not careful, people's approval can be my driver, and it can affect my mood in unhealthy ways.

My secondary temptation is ambition. I want to achieve great things. I want to be known as the best coach, the best writer, the best speaker. I am constantly comparing myself to others.

It's important to know your weaknesses so you can check your motives. For example, do you want to help somebody because you care or because you want them to like you? Are you simply enjoying your ice cream, or are you eating it to feel good about yourself and forget about your stress?

GREAT NEWS

We can overcome these temptations just as Jesus did in the wilderness. In all three instances Jesus went to God's Word to defeat Satan. How can we do the same?

Appetite is usually centered around fear. You worry that you won't have enough of something, so you consume. Money, food, alcohol, adventure, or information to feel better about yourself. In order to defeat appetite, we must be dependent on God and not on our own temporal things to fill the void in our heart. We need to go to God for protection and provision, instead of going to earthly things to fill our appetite.

A helpful verse: "I can do all things through him [Christ] who strengthens me" (Philippians 4:13).

Ambition is usually centered around guilt. You beat yourself up for feeling behind or wonder if you are doing the right activities for your life and business. You are constantly comparing your path to others. In order to defeat ambition, we need to be obedient to continue to hear God's word and direction for us. We have our own story. Our own life and career path. We must practice thanksgiving for what God has built into our life so far and where God has us this season.

A helpful verse: "Everyone then who hears these words of mine and does them will be like a wise man who built his house on the rock" (Matthew 7:24).

Approval can be centered around shame. You're always wondering if people like you. You are devastated when you find out someone is mad at you. People who struggle with the approval temptation often say yes when asked by others to do something in the hope they will like them more. In order to defeat approval, we need to embrace and understand that we are God's beloved. We are adored and approved by Him, thus we don't need the approval of others.

A helpful verse: "But to all who did receive him, who believed in his name, he gave the right to become children of God" (John 1:12).

In your next time of weakness, lean on God and His words to overcome that momentary temptation. By understanding your temptation, you can recalibrate to get back in the direction of what God is calling you to do.

11

HEAD TRASH

What Agreements Have You Made?

From when I was in high school to this day, I have loved downtown cities. I love buildings and development. The energy of something new, the signs of progress, the new architecture.

In high school (I remember this like it was yesterday) I told my college placement counselor I wanted to be an engineer. She advised me to find a different degree. I am going to assume the best about her, that her heart was in the right place, but the words I heard were, "You are not smart enough to be an engineer."

I went on to graduate with a civil engineering degree, and most semesters I was on the Dean's List. I became a licensed professional civil engineer and had a successful twenty-year career in the engineering and construction industry.

Why do I share this story? Because this is one of only a few times negative self-talk, what I call "head trash," played in my favor. I can't count how many times I didn't do something because of head trash. Didn't take the job. Didn't start the company. Didn't move internationally. Just didn't take action on an idea.

We all have our own head trash—that little voice that says we can't do it, we are not good enough. It may be something a parent told us that keeps haunting us today. Maybe it was a bully at recess from childhood or a coworker during a work project. Maybe it comes from a failure in our life that we keep replaying in our head.

Yes, sometimes these voices can motivate us to defeat them, but more times than not they hold us back.

WHAT IS YOUR HEAD TRASH?

A process that has been incredibly helpful to me and others is identifying key events in our life, both good and bad. Once you've identified these events, you can look for themes and agreements you have made. In chapter 8 I talked about agreements we have made with money, and they come into play here as well. As we look at events in our own life, we have made "agreements" with how that event has defined us in one way or another.

This exercise is helpful when you identify a minimum of three good and three bad events. Once you do, the agreements you have made will start to surface, and you will see the head trash that blows around in your mind.

Whenever we look at an event in our lives, we need to see the resulting lie or agreement we may have made. Instead of living with that agreement, we need to see the truth in the situation.

Here are a couple of personal examples.

Earlier I told you about my affair. For a long time, the resulting head trash I heard was that I was a failure, an imposter, a fraud. Until I came clean about my affair, this self-talk always haunted me. As with all agreements we make, they can prevent us from becoming who we were created to be. The agreement I made was that I was not good enough and would not be able to overcome this mistake. I didn't want to go to church because I knew about the skeleton in my closet. I wasn't vulnerable with people because I felt like a fraud since I was keeping a major secret. I was always reserved around Holly and scared I would get caught. I was not being my true self.

Once I came clean and accepted that I was forgiven by God, I could mentally begin the process of restoration. Restoration of my relationship with God, my wife, and myself.

The truth about my affair is I made a stupid and selfish mistake. I am not perfect. Since then I've made corrections in my life and continue to put up the appropriate boundaries to make sure it never happens again. The truth I live with now is I am not a fraud but a beloved son of God. I am a good husband and can lead my family well. I can invest in others and speak into their marriage because I am honest and vulnerable about my experience.

Another agreement I made in my life related to scarcity. I had to get student loans for college, and then I went through that real estate debacle in my early thirties. When I went through this exercise, I was shocked to see I was hanging onto the belief that I was the provider and God does not have my back. But I also saw how many times God did, in fact, show up to provide.

When I was a teenager, our church covered my parents' mortgage for a year as my mom fought cancer and my dad was unemployed. In college I received scholarships. When Holly and I moved to Cincinnati, we miraculously found a rental below market price in an excellent neighborhood. God provided during our process of coming out of debt from the real estate mess. All the coaching clients and experiences I have had in the last few years were people I didn't even know when I started this coaching journey.

God provided, not me. Yes, I have to steward well, but God is the provider.

Knowing that I am not the provider and God is, allows me to take more risks—to live more into His story and the greater adventure. This knowledge gave me the courage to leave corporate America to pursue the entrepreneurial life of a coach. And although I do worry some days, I am not paralyzed by finances.

What are the main stories in your life? What are the agreements you have made because of it?

- Did someone tell you that you were dumb and so you're slow to contribute ideas?

- Were you picked last in kickball as a kid and you still think about it?

- Did you pursue a new endeavor and fail so now you minimize risk?

- Were you betrayed by a friend and now are constantly on guard?

- Were you abused as a kid, whether verbal or physical, so you don't trust people?

- Did a parent walk out on your family so now you have feelings of abandonment?

- Were you told you were fat as a kid and have issues with food to this day?

Once we acknowledge the agreements we have made from our key stories, we can begin to overcome them. We overcome them by finding out the truth in the story and not the lie.

"DOGGONE IT, PEOPLE LIKE ME!"

About twenty years ago there was a very popular and funny skit on *Saturday Night Live* called "Daily Affirmation with Stuart Smalley." Stuart was a nerdy guy who used the power of verbal affirmations to make himself feel better. He looked in the mirror and said things like, "I am good enough, I am smart enough, and doggone it, people like me."

The reason SNL's skit was so popular was it related to something popular at the time—the rise of the self-help industry. People knew they needed positive self-talk, and this brought it out in the open, giving viewers a sense of relief. Then Stuart Smalley exaggerated the need to outrageous proportions, which made it hilarious.

Positive self-talk is on the rise again, which makes sense because words have power. God spoke to create Earth. Adam named the animals. Speaking out loud has greater power than just thinking a phrase. It gets us fired up when we say it out loud—like a rally cry.

I have mentors who do a daily verbal affirmation, so a few years ago I started to do it in times of doubt. It has been a game changer. When I am feeling defeated or hearing head trash, I go to God in prayer, but I also speak my affirmation out loud.

The following is an affirmation God laid on my heart during a season in which I was feeling a lot of shame and self-doubt. These are words I needed to hear: *I am a son of God. I am loved. Every day I am being called up and better equipped to connect people to greater performance and more significant purpose. I do not need the approval of others. I am approved and loved by God. I am a beloved son of God.*

I encourage you to write out a daily affirmation for you. Ask God to speak into your life about the words He has for you.

12

YOU FOLLOW ME!

Avoiding the Comparison Trap

Since beginning my journey from corporate America into leadership coaching, I've noticed a new area for me to compare myself to others—social media likes!

I wonder if people like the article I just posted. Do they like the video I made? I start to get excited about how many people "liked" something I posted, and then I see how many likes a Tony Robbins or Jon Gordon post is getting, and I feel defeated. Even though I know the statement from Jon Acuff, "Don't compare your beginning to someone else's middle," I can still hear the devil tell me I am behind, or people don't like what I am doing. I can do this with quantity of podcasts, speaking engagements, number of email subscribers, and the list goes on.

We do this in other ways as well. We compare our house size to somebody else's, their job title to ours, the way our kids behave compared to theirs, the type of car they drive, and on and on. If we are not careful, we allow the highlight reel of others to make us doubt who we are and where we are going.

Now comparison is not always bad. When comparison is used in a healthy way for inspiration and ideas, it's great! I love the book *Steal Like an Artist*, by Austin Kleon. It provides quotes and tips about getting inspiration from others and then adding your own voice and innovation to it. Austin talks about how good artists build on what has already been done before. Great art is just a combination of ideas already out there. You even see this in Scripture. Ecclesiastes 1:9 says, "There is nothing new under the sun." The key is to remain inspired and not defeated. Motivated and not jealous.

A WALK ON THE BEACH

Toward the end of chapter 21 in the Gospel of John is a story I find particularly helpful. To set the stage, we need to briefly look at the buildup to this point in John.

Peter has been following Jesus for a few years and is telling Jesus in John 13:37 that he will lay down his life for Him. Jesus responds that he will not; in fact, Jesus tells Peter he will deny Him three times. In the coming days Peter does just that.

Picking up at the end of John 21, Jesus has been crucified, risen from the dead, left the empty tomb, and is now on the beach. Jesus yells out to Peter and the other disciples while they are a little bit out to sea in a boat fishing. Peter is so excited to see Jesus that he jumps out of the boat and swims to shore! There at the beach an amazing restoration takes place as Jesus tells Peter He loves him three times—one for each of the denials!

Then something interesting happens. Jesus tells Peter how he is going to die. As they walk along the beach, the thought of dying is messing with Peter's head. Peter is already forgetting about the amazing restoration of his friendship with Jesus. He's consumed about how and when he will die.

At this point, in John 21:20, Peter sees another disciple on the beach (thought to be John by some), and he asks Jesus, "Well, what is going to happen to him?" Peter is comparing his death and remaining time to John's! Jesus quickly responds: "If it is my will that he remain until I come, what is that to you? You follow me!" Ouch.

Jesus is telling Peter, just like He tells each of us, to follow Him. What is it to us what others have or how their life is progressing compared to ours, or how long their good ride will last, or why their business is bigger, or why their title and responsibility are higher?

God has a story for each of us, and we are called to follow Him. We can look to others for inspiration and "steal their idea," but we must remember God has us here at this moment for a certain reason. There is an old, somewhat cheesy quote that is 100 percent accurate: "We must embrace the present, because it is a gift from God." So true.

Understanding we are part of a bigger story is a huge key in overcoming comparison.

GRATITUDE

Another key weapon against the battle of comparison is gratitude. Look over your shoulder and see how far you have come as we talked about in "Up and to the Right" in chapter 9. You may not be where some other people are, but they probably started at a different time than you. Or maybe you have different competencies. Who knows, you may leapfrog them, but it doesn't matter because you are in your own story, not theirs.

In times of frustration, hit pause and reflect on how far you have come. Give God thanks for all He has built in your life—the education, the jobs, the house, the adventure, the connections.

Through gratitude we can experience the joy of today. We can appreciate the beauty in the moment because we are not looking at others' lives.

If you feel like you are currently losing in the game of comparison, take time to reflect and journal about all the good you have in your life. What are you grateful for?

PART 2

MARRIAGE

"Submitting to one another out of reverence for Christ."

Ephesians 5:21

"Any marriage can be saved, and any marriage can be lost.
It all comes down to whether or not a couple will stop
doing the things that harm a marriage and start doing
the things that build a marriage."

JOE BEAM
Internationally recognized marriage expert

13

UNITED AS ONE

How to Have a Thriving Marriage

I was excited yet very nervous before my first coaching call with a new client. This was the largest contract I had ever received in my coaching career. The company hired me to do two one-on-one calls monthly with each executive, plus some group calls along the way. And I was about to have my first call with the president of the company, who was responsible for about two hundred employees.

The first call is always a discovery session in which I learn about the client personally and professionally. I ask questions and listen to the answers while being prayerful to discern where to go deeper based on his or her responses and tone. Based on the responses, I can get a sense of where the opportunities for growth are.

This client was giving great professional updates on how the business was growing, some recent hires they made, and the development of a new service they would be offering. The client was excited about the health of the company and the rapid growth over the last five years.

After discussing work for a few minutes, I wanted to learn about his personal life. Is he married? Does his wife work? How many kids do they have? What activities are they involved in? What part of the city do they live in? What church do they attend? Just trying to get a better understanding of his personal life and some of his story.

I then asked about the past weekend and what they did, and his tone started to change. All his weekend activities were about him and his kids. No mention of his wife. I remember earlier in the conversation he said in a confident and proud voice that he had been married for over twenty years, but his wife was never mentioned in the family activities.

I wondered why the updates didn't include his wife. Maybe she was out of town, but maybe there was more. Whenever I ask these direct and personal questions on coaching calls, it is always a risk because the person on the other end of the phone could shut down and not be transparent.

Instead, he started to open up and became very vulnerable, very quickly. He said they had not had "couple time" for the last few years. They had just been "doing family as a business." Although it saddened me to hear this, I was very grateful for his vulnerability. Knowing the state of the marriage, I had to press in.

Now pressing in with a client is always a risk, especially on the first call, because you don't know how they will respond. The risk here was he and his company hired me for leadership development for the business, so he may not have been ready or prepared to discuss his home life. But I believe firmly that leaders need to address personal issues in order for work to be sustainable, so I had to take the risk.

I was nervous. What if he terminates the contract on the spot? Will one of my largest contracts ever also be my shortest contract?

I went for it. I said, "You and your company hired me for business tools and leadership development, but before we do that, we need to address some of these issues at home first because they affect your work, whether you admit it or not."

There was a long pause! Was he getting ready to fire me? Was he getting ready to say just focus on the business piece, putting me in a moral dilemma?

Then he shocked me. "Yes, I know, because I get a pit in my stomach every day when I drive home from work." What?! A pit in the stomach!

This individual had tripled the business in the seven years he had been president, yet all the success at work could not help him overcome his daily pain on his way home. The wins at work do not counterbalance the losses at home.

WHAT ABOUT YOU?

Maybe your marriage is not as rocky as the one in this story, but without being intentional, you could end up here. Strong marriages take intentionality, vision, forgiveness, and love. A busy work season that requires travel or late nights could cause you and your spouse to drift. A rough series of months could lead to years of distance. We can then become complacent and start to think it just can't get any better.

However, when your marriage is strong, you have more to give as a leader. Your cup is full. We need to give our marriage the attention it needs and deserves. When our marriage is strong, the peaks of work feel even greater.

Your marriage can get better. It can start now.

A BETTER WAY

Over nineteen years of marriage, Holly and I have seen what

works for us, and of course what doesn't work. If we go too long without a date, we become like roommates. When we become selfish and are not serving each other, we both suffer. When we hold grudges instead of being quick to forgive, it creates a wedge between us.

The most important relationship in the home is the marriage, not the parent-to-child relationships. I don't think it is a coincidence that God put a husband and wife in the garden as the first relationship between two humans instead of a parent and child.

The best way to make sure you are thriving at home is to prioritize your relationship with your spouse. Some parents spend more time talking to their kids, thinking about their kids, or serving their kids than they do with their spouse. This can be a very slippery slope. Our intentions are good when we are loving our kids and wanting them to feel safe and valued. But the greatest gift we can give our kids is a healthy relationship between their mom and dad.

If we want our kids to feel safe and secure, a great start is for them to know they are from a loving relationship, for them to experience the oneness between their parents. If they see their mom and dad love each other, they feel safe. Kids have a sense of insecurity if they know the marriage of their parents is not secure. Kids know if they are in an unstable home.

The importance of investing time in our marriage seems obvious, yet our actions sometimes do not reflect this. For this to be our number-one relationship, we need to invest more time, thought, and energy here than in any other relationship.

Thriving marriages have these key elements that we will explore them in the following chapters:

- Serve Your Spouse
- Forgive Your Spouse
- Pursue Your Spouse

14

SERVING MINDSET

Do You Serve Your Spouse or Expect Your Spouse to Serve You?

A few years ago, our house had become a mess due to some busy travel weeks on my part as well as end-of-school-year activities. So we decided on a particular weekend it was time for some deep cleaning. Holly gave me the list of items she wanted me to clean, she had her list, and off we went.

A few hours later she noticed that some of the items on my list were still not done. So she asked me what I was doing. I proudly told her about all the hard work I was doing! I cleaned off all the dust from the ceiling fan blades throughout the house, I took off the floor and wall vents and cleaned them out. I even vacuumed the duct work that I could reach. I was so proud.

She was far from happy. None of those mattered to her. What she wanted clean were the items on the list. These were messes that had been annoying her and stressing her out over the past few weeks. Cleaning the bathroom, vacuuming the floor, dusting the dressers. That is what she wanted to have cleaned this weekend.

What happened is, as I started to work on the list Holly gave me, I saw some dirty areas that bothered me. Translation: I stopped serving her and the list she wanted done and instead served my own needs.

I like the quote that seasoned, wise married people say: "Is marriage a 50/50 split? No, it is 100/100." Both spouses need to be giving 100 percent to each other and to the marriage.

Serving your spouse is asking if they need anything while you are out running errands, encouraging your spouse to go out with their friends while you stay back and watch the kids. It's doing stuff you don't want to, like going out to see a romantic comedy or a sporting event. It's asking your spouse questions about their life and not always talking about your life.

SERVING IS HARD

When we are not happy with our spouses, serving is one of the first values to be thrown out the window. We tell ourselves they don't deserve it. They won't appreciate it, and I have better things to do anyway. When we start to go down that path, we start looking at other places where we get wins. If we think our spouse will not appreciate our actions, we go to work activities and spend time responding to emails, staying late at work, getting lost in the busyness. We occupy ourselves to justify not having the time to serve our spouse yet trying emotionally to get filled from our wins at work.

One of the greatest examples of overcoming this is to think about Jesus washing the feet of His disciples. Jesus had the humility and love to wash the feet of all His disciples, including Judas, who was about to betray Him.

We need to overcome our own pride and selfishness to love and serve our spouses.

SERVING MINDSET FLOWS INTO YOUR WORDS

In leadership trainings, we are often taught that "How can I help?' is a key question to motivate and encourage employees. This question lets your employees know you care yet also gets to the point of what is on their mind or is a bottleneck in their efforts.

The same is true in marriage. If our posture toward our spouse is "How can I help?" then it sets us up for success. It gives us a mindset of humility and service.

I see this play out often every weekend. When the weekend arrives, we all have our selfish desires, like going to the gym, going for a run, working on a project, or reading a book. We also have family commitments like soccer games, housework, and running errands.

Early on in my marriage, I would make sure my selfish list got done first. However, come Sunday night I would realize my wife really wanted something done. So there were times a tense conversation ensued, and I stayed up late Sunday night getting the project done.

When Holly and I are in our serving mindset, we talk on Friday night about what each of us really wants to get done that weekend. We both win. We both get our individual activities done, and the other person has their needs met as well. Instead of bitterness when one of us sees the other reading a book or going to the gym, there is peace because the agreed-upon tasks will still get done.

COMMUNICATE TO STOP THE DRIFT

One of the best words Holly and I added to our marital vocabulary is "roommate." Just saying that word to each other c be enough at times to get us to shake off the frustration and tr move into better relationship.

At times we tend to drift apart from our spouse. We may have a busy week of work travel, and when we come home, we are not clicking with our spouse. Then the weekend plans are busy with running errands and a few social gatherings. Then Monday comes and we start it all over again. If this rings true, you are not alone. Holly and I even joke about how the first twenty-four hours back from a work trip can be awkward and clunky, which makes it very hard if that extends over the weekend!

The difference between a good marriage and a great marriage is how long you allow the drift before you throw down the anchor and have a conversation. Two broken humans who are doing life together are going to have bad moments. When we put down the veneer of our perfect families and perfect marriages, we realize none of our families or marriages is perfect.

There are bad days, even bad weeks here and there. But the key to a great marriage is the recalibration of getting back on track. Otherwise we start to allow the drift, and then we start to justify the drift, which is even more dangerous, because it leads to us accepting the drift.

COMMUNICATE TO STAY ENGAGED

The best way to grow in your marriage is through talking about each other and not just about the kids. Talk to each other about your ups and downs, your goals and dreams, and also your frustrations and pain points. These conversations need to happen in the day to day.

One area of communication breakdown that is a microcosm of marriage communication in general is talking about work. A perfect example is when you and your spouse both come home from work and your spouse asks you how your day was. If you start a habit of saying "fine" or "same ol' same ol'," this can lead to days, weeks, months, even years when you are never communicating about work. Communication breakdown begins with each consecutive day you don't share.

If we give our spouses updates each day when they ask, they will be able to stay in tune to what we are doing. Whereas if you haven't kept them up to speed, you may feel like there is way too much to tell them, so you might just give up and not say anything.

The good news is it is never too late to start. You can start today by asking your spouse, "What happened today, and how did you feel?" Listen and interact, then provide your answer to that same question.

COMMUNICATE TO SHOW RESPECT

My wife is awesome in giving me the freedom to attend happy hours, go out for guys' nights, and accept random invitations I may get. Granted, she knows a lot of them are good for business since my business is built on relationships and referrals. But one thing is crucial to her willingness to let me go. Her attitude and mindset are dependent on whether I am asking or telling her that I am going to the happy hour. This is not because she wants control, but because she wants to know she matters. She wants to know I care about how my decision will impact her and her evening. The act of asking shows that I care about her.

I see this carry over into communicating about work travel. I ran into a guy at the gym recently who just got a new job in the last few months and had a lot of travel since starting the job. I asked about all the travel, and he said it has been hard, adding that he just got back the night before and was leaving the next day! He said he was too scared to tell his wife since he had just gotten back in town. Of course, the longer he waits, the madder she will be.

Travel for work is often necessary. You have to visit the client. You have to see the construction project. You need to train the branch office staff.

The question is, when do you tell your spouse about your travel schedule? I realize talking with your spouse about work travel can be difficult because it impacts the family schedule significantly. When you're gone, all the burdens of day-to-day family life (meals, cleanup, shuttling, doctor and dentist appointments, helping with homework, bedtime, etc.) fall to your spouse, and let's face it, the household workload can be heavy! No wonder this conversation can be tense.

Here's my advice: the time to talk to your spouse about your travel is as soon as you know you are traveling. Keep in mind the difficult conversation is likely to happen one way or another. But the longer you wait, the greater the argument.

I have traveled a lot at different times in my career. There was a time when I was gone every week Monday thru Friday as my colleagues and I were diligently working on a company sale. I have traveled internationally. These days I take ten-day trips to Montana a handful of times a year. I know the stress and weight is going to be heavy on Holly when I tell her, but the sooner I bring it up, the better, so she can mentally prepare and do any advance planning. The win is that she knows I am thinking about her and understand the inconvenience my trip is going to cause her.

Our spouses want to know they matter. Do you ask your spouse if you can go to the work happy hour, or do you tell him or her you are going?

You may get the same answer, but the manner in which you go about it either contributes to or subtracts from the long game of your relationship.

RECALIBRATION QUESTIONS

1. In the next week, how can you serve your spouse better?

2. Is there anything routine in his or her day that you can help with?

3. How can you shift your mindset to ask your spouse questions about their day and show interest in your spouse's life?

4. What schedule changes or trips do you have in the future that you need to communicate to your spouse?

5. How do they want to grow personally and professionally this year?

15

EVERYDAY FORGIVENESS

How Broken Image Bearers Thrive

Holly and I got home about the same time and met at the front door. I asked how the school meeting went, and she told me about an interaction with another parent. Holly felt the other parent had been rude and attacked her personally. Instead of just listening, I decided I needed to solve the problem. I wanted to coach her and give her some tips on how to handle conflict with another person.

She did not appreciate it, got mad, and walked away. Now I was mad. I was truly trying to help, and she walked away.

Now I had a choice. I could either hold a grudge and wait for her to apologize, or I could go tell her I was sorry and ask for her forgiveness. This time I chose correctly. I swallowed my pride and apologized.

One reason a wedge develops between spouses is we allow our negative thoughts to build up each day. Almost like a snowball rolling down the hill, we allow more and more negative thoughts to pile on until all we see is this big snowball of mistakes.

God does not do that to us. If we are to be image bearers of God in our marriages, then we must not do it either. We all know we should apologize and forgive our spouses, yet we struggle.

DON'T LET YOUR ANGER BUILD UP

I remember a few years ago Holly and I got into an argument. Our kids overheard it, and they were crying as they told us they didn't want us to get a divorce. I don't even remember what we were arguing about (that's often the case, right?). It was something very small, but we had allowed frustration to build up so that one small thing became the straw that broke the camel's back.

A verse that has been helpful in my life and my marriage is Lamentations 3:22–23: "The steadfast love of the Lord never ceases; his mercies never come to an end; they are new every morning; great is your faithfulness."

Every day we get new mercies! Every day is a new day. We get a clean slate. God does not keep score of what we did yesterday and carry it over to this day. Nor should we. Every day in our marriage should be a new day of new mercies for our spouse.

THE BRUTAL FACTS

When working with clients, we talk about how we need to be honest with current work conditions. When doing so, we use a concept by Jim Collins in *Good to Great* that great companies and leaders confront the brutal facts yet have an unwavering hope for the future. We need this same perspective for our marriage. We need to confront the brutal facts yet have an unwavering hope for the future.

The brutal fact is that we and our spouses are not perfect. We are broken. Our attitudes are not perfect. We make mistakes—lots of them. So the first step is to come to grips with the current reality of the situation. Once you confront the brutal facts, then embrace the realization that with effort there is great hope for the future in your marriage.

It's important to remember there are strong marriages out there that overcame greater valleys than you are currently experiencing.

- Couples who have filed for bankruptcy and now are financially thriving
- Couples who have survived not one, two, three bouts of infidelity but double digits, and yet now they are thriving
- Couples who have separated and are now back together

This is not a hall pass to do what you want, but it's reassuring to know other couples have overcome greater challenges in their marriage than what you need to overcome.

VIEW YOUR SPOUSE AS GOD DOES

In the first couple years of marriage, this was pretty easy. Right after getting married, our spouse still seemed perfect, and the newness of the marriage, honeymoon, and starting life together was all happening.

But as time passes, we realize our spouse is not perfect. We quickly brush off the fact that we are not perfect, but we take careful notice of our spouse's imperfections. On bad days, we see our *intentions* while taking careful stock of our spouse's imperfections.

If we were true image bearers of God in our marriage, we would see our spouses as God sees them—as a beloved daughter or beloved son of God. Their shortcomings would not be our focus.

When we look at our spouses, we need to realize they are broken and not perfect. We need to take their weaknesses for granted and notice their strengths. What we often do, instead, is take their strengths for granted and notice their weaknesses.

Pray each morning that you will view your spouse as God

views him or her. Our love for our spouse should never cease, and mercies are new every morning.

THREE TYPES OF FORGIVENESS

The definition of forgiveness is when we release being wronged and do not require the person to pay a debt. Forgiveness is releasing the past so you can focus on the future. Without forgiveness, we are tethered to the past. We are allowing the hurt from our spouse's action to control our attitude going forward.

Yet there are various degrees of forgiveness.

One extreme is the small events that happen to us and we immediately forgive and do not give it much thought. Our spouse did not do what he or she agreed to do, didn't help around the house, forgot to pick something up at the grocery store, didn't reply to a text. Our spouse will do something to frustrate us, yet we quickly forgive them and move on. These are minor, almost a nonevent.

The other extreme is when something huge happens. A major act of betrayal. An affair. Running up credit card debt. A physical or verbal outburst. Pornography. Drug use. The forgiveness process is not always as simple as "I am sorry," "OK, you are forgiven."

Jesus commands us to forgive even in these instances, yet there may still be consequences for the individual's actions. However, the purpose of this chapter is not to lay out the grieving and restoration process. There are other sources for that. My only comment here is that there is hope for overcoming any of those major sins. I speak from experience of how my wife forgave me, but I am also aware of numerous other amazing restoration stories. I will say, the only ones I am aware of that were successful had God at the center of the healing process. Two people alone can't do it.

The area of sin I want to address here is in the middle. A little bigger than something we can brush off, yet not extreme. A snarky negative comment our spouse makes. Going against something you two have agreed on in your parenting. Some poor financial decisions behind your back. I see couples get into trouble here because they think they can just brush it off. Yet over time a major wedge is built between two people.

It is the compound effect of many of these "small" sins that create the major distance. This major distance is when people lose hope in their marriage.

However, this can be avoided if we speak up early and often. We must step in and confront the situation. Otherwise, every action or comment our spouse makes will be seen through this lens of frustration and bitterness.

A trigger for me when I realize I am holding onto something is when Holly says, "I can't do anything right today." The reality is, she probably is doing everything similar to other days, but that day I am viewing her through a lens of frustration.

COMMUNICATE TO FORGIVE

The first step is to identify what is frustrating you and then begin the forgiving process.

Forgiving is also more than just saying in your mind, "I forgive," or writing it in your journal. Instead, it is important to communicate with your spouse about the situation. If you are in the wrong, then it is admitting you are wrong and apologizing. If your spouse is in the wrong, tell your spouse you forgive him or her. The devil loves unspoken frustrations. When we let them sit in our mind, they begin to multiply, so we must communicate.

Communication is a big part of the forgiveness process. Jesus tells us in Matthew 5:24 to go and "be reconciled with your brother," and in Matthew 18:15 to "go and tell him his fault."

Once you identify the issue and communicate with your spouse, you need to release it and not bring it up again. This is easier said than done because as you release it and step forward, the devil wants to keep reminding you of the action. If we sit in our bitterness and keep replaying the action, then it keeps us from growing and moving forward.

In Ephesians 6, Paul is talking about putting on the "armor of God" as a way to defeat evil. One of the pieces of armor is the "belt of truth," which is the truths in Scripture. When you are feeling the old thoughts creep in, then the following verses can be helpful to have as your armor:

- Colossians 3:13, "As the Lord has forgiven you, so you also must forgive."

- Ephesians 1:7, "In him we have redemption through his blood, the forgiveness of our trespasses, according to the riches of his grace."

RECALIBRATION QUESTIONS

1. As you read this chapter, there probably was a prick in your spirit about something your spouse has done to you that you still have not forgiven him or her for. What is it? Now is the time to forgive your spouse for it, as we have also been forgiven by Jesus.

2. What do you need to release from your mind that your spouse has done?

3. Similarly, as you read this, did you feel guilty of an action that you have never completely apologized for from the heart? Maybe it is something you said. Maybe it is something you did. Say you are sorry to your spouse for whatever is coming to mind.

16

PURSUE YOUR SPOUSE

Are You Intentional with Your Spouse?

One of the major reasons for my affair earlier in our marriage is Holly and I stopped dating each other. We went out together all the time, but it was in groups or double dates. We stopped being intentional with one another. We stopped making time to ask each other questions about ups and downs, hopes and dreams. In the moment I didn't realize what was happening because we were spending time together, but it was rarely just the two of us.

Many of us know date nights are important, but through the busyness of life, it is often one of the first activities we drop. We are tired, it costs money, and the excuses pile up. We are all guilty of saying we had a long week at work and just want to stay in, watch TV, order pizza, and hang with the kids. That is great sometimes, but if it continues for a long period of time, before you know it, you have not been on a date for months, and you're living as roommates.

In order to have a healthy and thriving marriage, dates should be a nonnegotiable. We need to connect with our spouses, understand what is going on in their world, what they are processing, how they are doing, what is on their radar in the months to come—most importantly, what is on their heart. Without dates, we just go from day to day, activity to activity, and we don't have conversations that go deeper than schedule management.

DON'T WAIT FOR LATER

In one of my workshops a woman said she and her husband don't go on dates. It is just the season they are in, she said. They will go on dates later.

Sometimes later never comes because marriages without dates don't last. If a dateless marriage does last, it will be a lukewarm marriage at best. And if a couple does beat the odds, what will they even talk about on the date when they are older? Years have passed without talking to each other about the things that matter most, so the desire to connect may not be there.

Another reason date night is often cancelled is that it costs money. Yes, going out to eat, having some drinks, and paying a babysitter adds up, but I guarantee the costs of dates are much cheaper than marriage counseling and especially divorce attorney fees. We need to do our best to push through and have the date, even if it means doing it on the cheap with nachos and beer. The important part is connecting, looking at each other, and having fun.

One of my favorite date nights with Holly happened when we first moved to Cincinnati. We had just moved from Denver and were in a very tight financial situation because we had decided for Holly to quit her job, forgoing a nice salary, so she could stay home with the kids. Living on a small budget, yet knowing we had to go on a date, we went to a bar, had nacho appetizers for our meal, a couple beers, and sat on a rooftop. It was very low budget, but our intentionality and the fact that we both made the sacrifice to be together made for a special night and a great memory. I still smile when I drive by that sports bar.

Date night for us is now a nonnegotiable. We have two dates a month, sometimes more, but never less. If this is a growth area for you, I encourage you to start planning a date night a few times a month.

HAVE FUN TOGETHER

The best way to build stability in your marriage is through friendship. When you hear people, who have been in a healthy marriage for thirty or more years, they often say the reason for their strong marriage is that their spouse is their best friend. So how do we do that?

You love to watch sports, but your wife doesn't. You love to sew and be creative, but your husband doesn't. People tell me that it is hard because they don't like the same stuff as their spouse. I agree, yet that doesn't stop us with our other friends!

Some of my close friends love golf. I don't like golf. So we don't golf together, but we do other things. We trail run and go to FC Cincinnati soccer games. We find things we both enjoy doing.

The same goes for your spouse. Don't focus on what one of you doesn't like to do. Find what you both love to do together and do it! Make time for it. If you don't know what you both like, start trying things out. Go to cooking classes, go on a hike, try tennis, go to concerts, go on a bike ride.

Through activities and adventure with our spouse, we can build a friendship that will help carry the marriage during tough times.

WE DRIFTED

Holly and I had a once-in-a-lifetime vacation a few years ago, an all-expenses-paid trip aboard a private yacht in the British Virgin Islands. According to the couple who lived on the yacht and served as our cooks and tour guides, Robert DeNiro slept in our bed the previous week! Pretty amazing.

Here we are in one of the most beautiful places in the world, so we were excited for some adventure! We decided to do something we had never done—go scuba diving. In the British Virgin Islands, you could get certified to scuba dive by passing the certification process there on site. This included underwater breathing tests in the swimming pool. Once certified, you then would go out to sea for a two-hour scuba dive.

Long story short, the pool part didn't go too well for me. I freaked out. Even though the water was only eight feet deep, I kept thinking I would take a deep breath and all this water would come gushing in. The lady doing the certification process was so kind and kept letting me retry, but finally she had to say I was not able to be certified. She knew that if I was this scared in shallow water with zero fish, what would happen in the ocean?!

Holly, on the other hand, passed her test and ran over to share her excitement. Quickly her happiness turned to frustration. It was my idea to spend the time and money to go scuba diving as a couple, but I failed the test. After seeing her excitement, I decided we should go out to sea, she could scuba dive, and I would sit on the boat and watch.

I swallowed my pride, and we rode out to sea with the rest of the group. Everybody with their scuba gear ready to dive except me. I was just in my swimsuit and shirt. I felt like a loser. Plus, the tension was growing greater between Holly and me, as we were spending this time and money for an activity only one of us could do.

After our ride out to sea, it was time for everybody to jump into the ocean to scuba dive. By this point I was looking forward to this time, so I could get a break from the tension. Maybe if Holly saw some beautiful fish, this would all be better for her and me.

Well, it didn't go as planned. As Holly jumped in and went under water, she freaked out. Whether she got scared she was going to get eaten by a fish, or breathe in water instead of air, she decided she was done.

So there we sat. Hundreds of dollars down the drain, not to mention the lost opportunity for other activities we could have pursued. Sitting on a nasty boat, frustrated at each other for the whole situation, and forced to sit there and watch everybody have the time of their life scuba diving.

Holly and I had a choice. We could continue to fester in our anger, disappointment, and judgement. Or one of us could break the ice, choose to forgive and have grace for each other, and enjoy the moment.

I don't remember who broke the ice, but I remember we both made a conscious decision to change our mindsets. We ended up enjoying our couple of hours at sea, and we now look back fondly at that memory.

Sometimes circumstances get in the way of having fun together, but even then, with intentionality we can pull it off.

RECALIBRATION QUESTIONS

1. When is your next date scheduled?

2. Do you have a vacation planed for just you two this year?

3. If you can't do an evening date, then when can you do a Saturday morning breakfast together?

4. What is something fun you two could do together in the next month? Tennis, canoe, sporting event?

PART 3

PARENTING

*"Whoever spares the rod hates his son,
but he who loves him is diligent to discipline him."*

Proverbs 13:24
(footnote in ESV adds, *"He who loves him disciplines him early."*)

*"If you don't lead people someplace good, someone will lead
them someplace bad. The worst thing a parent can say about
raising their kids is—I don't want to tell them what to do.
I want them to figure it out on their own. The moment you
create a void in direction is the moment that someone else fills
that void. If they fill it with something bad or that contradicts
your values and vision—you are in trouble."*

DONALD MILLER
Author, speaker, and CEO of StoryBrand

17

DECLARE YOUR KIDS' IDENTITY

The Power of a Coming-of-Age Celebration for Your Children

In Matthew 28:19–20 we are called to go and make disciples. A lot of us are familiar with this verse, and we tend to think it applies only outside the home. We spend a lot of time looking for people to go and build into, but if we're not careful, we can completely overlook our own kids!

Intentional investments into our kids will have a greater impact than anything else we do. Kids want our time more than anything. Our presence over our provision. Yes, they love their iPhones and tablets, but often they are playing with those because we are not giving them attention. Do you blame them? We do the same thing. When we are at stoplights, in lines, and even on the toilet, we are on our phones. Our kids are like us.

We need to go out on dates with our kids and do what they want so they feel loved, plus we get to know them better. Yes, there can be some valuable time talking and driving around together, whether we're going on errands or to and from their activities, but the real value for them is when they know we are taking time out of our schedule to be with them.

For my teenage daughter, it is going to Starbucks and talking. For my younger kids, it's going out for ice cream or a donut. It doesn't matter where as long as it is a time in which you are being intentional with your kids. In our family, the goal is do at least one date per month per kid.

Parenting is about intentionality with our children, so they know who they are and whose they are, guiding them in what to do with their life and helping shape how to live it out.

As adults, we all have struggled to better understand our identity. If it is hard for us, think how hard it is for our kids! As parents, we need to be proactive and speak into our kids' identities. If we don't guide them properly, somebody else will, and they could end up making similar mistakes as we have, or worse.

DESIGNING A COMING-OF-AGE CELEBRATION

A few summers ago, our daughter Kiley turned thirteen, and we wanted to celebrate her transition from a little girl to a young lady. Obviously, coming-of-age celebrations are not a new concept. One thinks of the Bat/Bar Mitzvah, tribal-type ceremonies in other countries, and the over-the-top celebrations on MTV's *My Sweet 16*. But Christians and nonreligious people don't really have a standard coming-of-age celebration.

In addition, when my wife and I were looking for coming-of-age ceremonies, we found great information for a father to do with his son or for a mother to do with her daughter.

But we couldn't find anything for fathers and daughters or both parents and a daughter.

Stories and studies demonstrate that when children lose their way in life, it often can be traced back to a wound from their earthly father abandoning, ignoring, or abusing them. Later in life they try to fill the father void with sex, work, food, drugs, etc.

My wife and I wanted to put a stake in the ground. We wanted to affirm who our daughter is, that she is defined by her identity as a daughter of God, not by how many social media likes she has or whether boys ask for her phone number or whether she's the best dancer at her studio. We wanted her to know she is living *from* a place of approval instead of *for* approval.

Our ceremony was a combination of resources and ideas from organizations we are involved in or that we came across during preparation. The New Frontier I mentioned earlier has fathers and sons participate in an impactful ceremony during the father/son weeks in Montana (thenewfrontierministries.org). Also, Senior Pastor Brian Tome of Crossroads Church in Cincinnati did an incredible sermon series and has written a book on *The Five Marks of a Man*, which includes five significant ways men are different from boys. Again, we were able to incorporate some of this material. The close of our ceremony came from an amazing story in Exodus 38 that I heard author Kate Battistelli talk about on the radio one morning.

In addition to these resources, my wife and I studied Proverbs 31, which is rich with words and traits of a godly woman. We identified five specific words we felt were significant to a young lady transitioning into a young woman that were applicable to our daughter at this time in her life. If we do this ceremony again when she is older, we may pick other words that are applicable to her at eighteen, such as "entrepreneur" or "business minded." We may also pick different words for our second daughter, such as "creative," since she is wired for art and creativity.

Following are the five words from Proverbs 31 that embody who Kiley is at this time and what we felt God wanted us to affirm in her:

- **CHARACTER**—trustworthiness, integrity, wisdom, and kindness (vv. 10–12)

- **COMMITTED**—to faith, family, friends, school, and work (vv. 13–19)

- **GENEROUS**—of time, talent, and treasures (vv. 20–22)

- **INFLUENTIAL**—live a life worth imitating (vv. 23–26)

- **EXCELLENCE**—everything you do is for the Glory of God (vv. 27–31)

We then asked some family members and close friends to write a letter to Kiley based on one of the five words. We assigned each person the one word we thought they lived out the most and asked them to write a letter about what this word means to them. For the men involved, we also asked them to share how they see it played out in a godly woman. For the women, we asked them to reflect on how the assigned word has affected their life and to offer any wisdom they could share with a thirteen-year-old girl.

We then put all the letters in a beautiful bound book with pictures from throughout Kiley's life. I cannot tell you how amazing the book is! The treasure of the book in itself is worth doing the ceremony! We often joke that we could sell this book on Amazon and just substitute the name of the customer for our daughter's name. The book is full of incredible insight and wisdom.

I invited the men who wrote a letter to come to our house around 4:00 p.m. on her birthday and discuss the words with our daughter. I'm not going to lie; it started off a little awkward with Kiley at the head of the dining room table and these grown men sitting around the table and staring at her. But after a few awkward minutes it burst open with greatness. We discussed each word for about fifteen minutes, the guys read their letters, and we prayed over her.

Now, will she remember all the great things these men said that night? Absolutely not. I don't even remember. But she will always have their letters, and she will not forget there are godly men who can speak into her life, help her out when needed, or just be prayer warriors working behind the scenes for her. She knows she is not alone.

The next part of the celebration was when my wife and I took her to a fancy dinner that evening. We got dressed up, ate a nice meal, celebrated her, and we each shared our thoughts with her based on the five words. The dinner was special. Laughs and tears.

Then we came back home. Now it was Holly and a group of women sitting around the table with Kiley, and they did the same thing. The ladies talked about the five words, ate dessert, and had a great time.

BURN YOUR MIRRORS

The last part of our night was the perfect close to an amazing evening. Holly and I have participated in a ceremony called "Burn Your Ships" at Crossroads Church, which is based on a story from the 1500s when Captain Hernán Cortés landed in Veracruz and told his crew to burn their ships because they were not going to retreat. I have always liked this idea of burning your ships or fears or whatever is holding you back, so when I heard this story from Kate Battistelli on Exodus 38:8, I knew we had to include it in our ceremony.

The Bible tells us the Israelite women were asked to burn their bronze mirrors so the liquid metal could be used in constructing the washbasins at the tabernacle. Kate said this illustrates that while women are beautiful and reflect God's glory, how women look should not define their self-image or come before their identity as God's daughter.

We gave Kiley a bronze mirror and a marker to write on it anything she was struggling with, that was getting in the way of her relationship with God or just holding her back from living life to the full. I don't know what she wrote on the mirror because it was private, but I am sure it had to do with pressure to get perfect grades, social media likes, getting a boyfriend, being a great dancer, and the list goes on. After she was done writing, we had her throw it in the fire!

After she threw the mirror in the fire, we watched it burn, symbolizing that all those fears and worries were burned. They do not define her. We celebrated and then gave her a new bronze mirror with the five words from the ceremony embroidered on the mirror frame!

The evening was amazing.

We must affirm our kids for who they are now and cast a vision for who they can become, not what the noise of the world is telling them. Somebody is building into your kids. Make your voice louder than the others.

MORE THAN JUST A DAY

Kiley's coming-of-age celebration was an amazing experience, but it happened over the course of one day. Obviously, declaring our children's identities is not just a one-day project. Once we had the ceremony, it was critical to continue with regular investments.

Kiley and I go on dates and discuss how she is living out the five words in her life as well as how she is living as a daughter of God. When Holly and I see her exemplifying a positive character trait, we affirm her. When Kiley is deflated due to a bad test result or unsatisfactory dance recital, we remind her that she is not defined by her tests results or dance ranking, but instead she is a daughter of God. Similarly, if she gets first place and pride creeps in, no question we are there to cheer her on, but over time we also discuss the risks of tying identity to temporal success.

Without the regular investments, the temptations of how the world defines failure and success will start to creep in and affect Kiley's mindset. The identity ceremony requires follow up to provide transformation and lifelong impact, otherwise it is just an inspirational night and nice memory.

NEVER TOO EARLY OR TOO LATE

Some of you may be thinking your kids are too young, or maybe you think you missed the boat because your kids are in their twenties.

It is never too early or too late!

For those with young kids, how amazing to be learning about the importance of identity at this age in your child's life. Our kids' identity needs to be tied to character, values, and mindset instead of their achievements (straight A's, goals scored in a soccer game, etc.). As you compliment your kids at this young age, be sure to compliment their character over their competency. Compliment their values over their outcomes.

Getting this right now will set them up for success later.

You are also never too *late* to affirm your kids' identity! Even if they are out of the house or already married, it is not too late. All children need to have their identity spoken over them, especially by their parents.

At The New Frontier we will get a father in his fifties or sixties with his son in his twenties or thirties, and to have that father speak over his son is always a tear jerker for me. Nothing can make a young man feel so vulnerable, yet honorable, as to hear words of affirmation and identity spoken over him by his earthly father.

LESSONS FROM THE #METOO MOVEMENT

In recent years women have begun reporting high-powered men who sexually abused or harassed them in their Hollywood, business, or news media careers. This became known as #MeToo Movement because female victims were using social media and the #MeToo hashtag as a way to build awareness.

Affirming our kid's identity is critical for many reasons, one of which is that our kids are tomorrow's leaders. We need to be correctly affirming their identity, so they can humbly yet confidently lead and not be a prey or the predator in sexual harassment, racial or gender discrimination, or other abuses of power in the workplace.

We need to affirm our sons' identities, so they do not slip throughout life and end up being a predator—looking for affirmation of who they are, trying to fill a void in their heart, and pursuing immediate gratification. We need to affirm our daughters' identities too, so they can have the self-confidence and self-esteem to avoid compromising situations.

RECALIBRATION QUESTIONS

1. Which of your kids need to have their identity affirmed?

2. How and when will you do the identity ceremony?

3. How have you complimented your children's character over their competency lately?

18

HELPING OUR CHILDREN THRIVE

Managing the Tension between Invitation and Challenge

As we pursue relationships with our spouse, kids, friends, and even employees, there is a natural and inherent tension between nurturing a good relationship on the one hand and pursuing the relevant responsibilities on the other. Let me share a few examples.

For married couples with children, the tension may be between intimacy, being husband and wife, growing old together, and laughing on the one hand, and yet stewarding money well, impacting others, and raising kids on the other.

With kids, the tension is often between building relationship, going on parent-child dates, throwing the ball around in the backyard, and just being a friend on the one hand, and yet needing to encourage them to get decent grades in school, discipling them, and make smart choices on the other.

With friends, the tension is often between having fun, laughing, and attending events that your spouse doesn't enjoy on the one hand, and yet holding them accountable and speaking truth into their life when you see them going off course.

This tension carries over to our work when we have employees with whom we need to have a relationship, but we also have a job to do.

I coach a Chief Financial Officer of a 300-employee company, so he has a lot of big decisions to make on a daily basis. Our coaching calls are an hour long, and on one particular call I could tell he was not engaged. His mind was elsewhere. Plus, he usually comes to every call prepared with notes and updates to give me. So about fifteen minutes into this call, I asked him, "What is the matter? You are not as engaged as usual." He said, "Nothing." I said, "We need to talk about it because it is impacting you right now, and I know it is impacting the rest of your work. What is it?"

He said, "It's no big deal. It is not work related." I said, "Even though it is not work related, it is affecting your work, so we should talk about it."

He eventually opened up and said their ten-year old daughter was causing them challenges at home. He and his wife didn't feel they were making any headway with her.

Don't miss this: a CFO of a large company is not able to concentrate at work because he is not connecting well with his child at home! In order to win at work, we have to win at home first.

INVITATION AND CHALLENGE

After listening to him talk, I shared with him the Invitation vs. Challenge matrix, which I learned a few years prior from Five Capitals. This is one of my favorite tools because it is applicable and effective in any leadership and relational role, whether at home or work.

Although the tool is simple to understand, it needs constant evaluation to make sure you are correctly calibrated for the situation. The Invitation part of the matrix is all about inviting a person into a relationship—spending time with and getting to know him or her. The Challenge part of the matrix is all about challenging them into responsibility. There is a job to get done or a responsibility to look after, and you as the leader of the home or at work need to see that it gets done.

We see Jesus model this as He invites the disciples to spend time with Him. "Come follow me," He says, yet He challenges them with, "Go and make disciples." In almost every encounter Jesus has with people, you'll see this balance of grace and truth, relationship and responsibility, invitation and challenge. In John 4 He invites the woman at the well to have living water yet challenges her by saying she has had five husbands and the man she currently lives with is not her husband. In Matthew 19:16–22 He invites the rich young ruler to follow Him yet challenges him to sell all of his belongings.

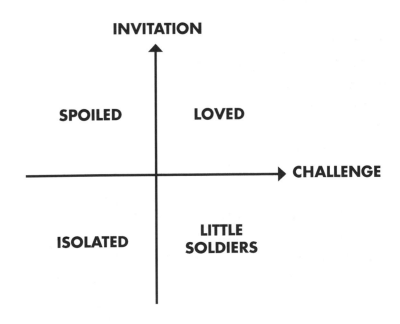

This tool works very well at home and work, but for the sake of this chapter, we will unpack each quadrant from the lens of the parent and child. When we are all Challenge as a parent, and minimal Invitation, we're like a dictator. This is the bottom right quadrant of the matrix. All we care about is making sure our kids are getting the job done—getting good grades, making their bed, reading their daily devotions, doing their chores. We don't ever let down our guard and just play with them or just talk. We are always in "parent mode," driving for results. Our kids feel like little soldiers just marching to our directions, and they feel lonely.

This can look like controlling behavior. We are very busy with work, can't always be around our kids, so at times we can be controlling so that our kids don't screw up. Maybe because we know the dumb mistakes we made at their age, or we don't want the embarrassment to our family name, or we just don't want to see our kids hurt. We can sometimes overswing and use control as a parenting tool.

But control is not the answer. Control backfires when they get out of the house and decide to go "sow their oats" or go explore ways to break free of the controlling environment. Instead of control, we want to provide freedom within a framework. I'm not talking about framework as just rules and regulations, but instead a framework of values, principles, and purpose.

For the bottom left quadrant, you just are absent. No Invitation, no Challenge. Your kids will feel very isolated in this state. If you are taking the time to read this book, you are most likely not in this quadrant.

The other common quadrant is the upper left quadrant, where it is all Invitation and minimal Challenge. In this quadrant we just want to be our kids' best friend. We create a cozy environment. As the parent, we are always saying yes to their requests. Yes, you can have that candy. Yes, you can have that toy. Yes, you can spend the night at your friend's house. Our reason for saying yes may vary from time to time. Sometimes we say yes because we are tired and yes is the easy button, while other times we say yes because we want to be liked or be cool. This behavior also looks like always letting the kid make the choice for the family on where to go out to eat or even commitment choices such as whether they want to go to practice or stay home.

We all know parents like this, and growing up we loved our friends who had parents like this because we got to do whatever we wanted. I learned how to drive a car before I was legally allowed to because of a cozy parent of a friend of mine! We have a word for kids in this category: spoiled. These kids develop an entitled mindset that will carry over into their adult life.

We were not made for a cozy environment. We were made to thrive. As Jesus says in John 10:10, we were made for life to the full. A full life is one that has relationship and responsibility. Relationship with those in our lives plus the responsibility to be productive. God commanded us in Genesis 1 to be fruitful and multiply but also to subdue the earth and have dominion over it—relationship and responsibility. Invitation and Challenge.

When we are leading with both Invitation and Challenge, we are empowering those who are under our leadership, whether at home or in the office. When kids are led with both Invitation and Challenge, they feel loved, and employees feel valued and empowered.

Think through those you lead at home and work and plot on this matrix how you are currently leading them. Are they in the correct quadrant? Is it time to recalibrate and bring more Invitation into the relationship or more Challenge?

SHARING THE TOOL WITH YOUR KIDS

I encourage you to share this matrix tool both with your employees and with your children so they can better understand your mindset. I have shared it with hundreds of people, but my favorite was sharing it with my daughter a few years ago.

That particular week Kiley, ten years old at the time, kept asking us for things, and we kept saying no. She asked us for a sleepover. We were not opposed to it in principle, but that weekend was not a good time. She asked us to go to King's Island (an amusement park) with her friends and no adults; we were not OK with that. There were a few other no's we said that week, and she got frustrated with us. "You guys always say no!" she told us.

This fired me up! But instead of just arguing about it or ignoring it and walking away, I decided to have a teaching moment using this tool.

I drew the matrix, gave her a high-level overview of the lines and meanings of the words, and then we discussed each quadrant. We discussed what it would look like if we always said no, so I brought up things we had said yes to, such as other sleepovers, so she realized she wasn't deprived. When she agreed we were not operating in that quadrant, we moved to the top left quadrant.

If we always said yes, we discussed, then she would feel entitled and spoiled. We mentioned some of her friends who are in that category and how their behavior plays out, and she acknowledged this wasn't the right answer either.

We then talked about how we wanted our parenting to provide both fun and discipline. Relationship and responsibility. The reason for that is we want her to feel loved and protected.

Yes, she was still disappointed we said no, but now she had a better understanding of why we made the decisions we did.

WHY THIS IS SO IMPORTANT

In Angela Duckworth's book *Grit: The Power of Passion and Perseverance*, she has a chapter on "Parenting for Grit." In that chapter she builds a case of Invitation vs. Challenge. She calls it Supportive vs. Demanding. One data point she shares is from psychologist Larry Steinberg. In his 2001 presidential address to the Society for Research on Adolescence, he proposed a moratorium on further research on supportive and demanding parents because he believed there was overwhelming evidence for the importance of combining the two styles.

In one particular study by Larry Steinberg, he had ten thousand American teenagers complete a questionnaire about their parents' behavior. Angela Duckworth summarized these test results in *Grit*: "Regardless of gender, ethnicity, social class, or parents' marital status, teens with warm, respectful and demanding parents earned higher grades in school, were more self-reliant, suffered less anxiety and depression, and were less likely to engage in delinquent behavior."

Wow. That's reason enough to consider how to parent in the top right quadrant, of both Invitation and Challenge.

Proverbs 13:24 says, "Whoever spares the rod hates his son, but he who loves him is diligent to discipline him." What a bold verse. I think we all have seen parents who don't discipline their kids. We ourselves may take the passive approach when we are tired or busy, but this verse says when we do this, we "hate" our children. The idea is that if we love our children, we will do what's best for them, which is discipline them.

Talking with a friend about this verse, he brought up a point that I had always overlooked. The English Standard Version has a footnote that says, "He who loves him disciplines him early." Disciplining our kids when they are young is so critical because it sets the stage for the years to come. Don't be overprotective when your kids are little, because that is when discipline makes the most impact.

A few months ago, we got a new dog, a Shih Tzu, and it was biting our kids in the face. As you can imagine, this was very stressful because we had this cute puppy, all of our kids wanted to pet it, but Zoar kept biting them. We were getting close to having to give it away, so Holly looked online to see if there were any last-ditch efforts we could make to stop the dog from biting.

Come to find out, small dogs like a Shih Tzu do what is called "nipping." Although it is still a form of biting, it is a quick snap of the jaw. One of the reasons Shih Tzu's nip is because of "improper hierarchy." They believe they are the alpha of the house. We followed some tips from the website such as not letting the dog run ahead on a walk and being the first one through the door when going on a walk. After we did this for a few weeks, Zoar stopped nipping! He understood his role in the family.

The same holds true for our kids. We can allow them to nip by not discipling them early enough, or we can establish the parent/child hierarchy by using discipline at a young age.

RECALIBRATION QUESTIONS

Plot each of your family members in the Invitation/Challenge quadrant that you currently have them in. Do you need to recalibrate?

1. If they are in the bottom right quadrant (all Challenge), is it time to take your foot off the gas and go have fun with them and ask how they are doing?

2. If they are in the top left quadrant (all Invitation), is it time to challenge them into responsibility in house chores, school performance, or other areas?

19

PARENTAL TONE

The Kind of Parents We Want to Be— Honest and Fun

We have all walked into houses where we have immediately felt on edge. When we were kids, we knew if we did something wrong, the parents of that house would get mad. Now as a parent, when I walk into a house like that I am on eggshells, scared my kids will break something or do something wrong. A tension is in the air, and nobody wants to cause the eruption. Don't ask the wrong question, say the wrong thing, or do the wrong action.

On the other hand, there are houses we have all walked into and thought, "What a fun place." Music is playing, family members are laughing, everyone is engaged, and there is a good energy in the air.

Every house has a culture, and just like in companies, the

leader sets the culture. The term we use to define culture in the home is "parental tone," since the parents create the culture in a home. The parental tone that Holly and I try to practice is defined by honesty and fun.

SOURCE OF TRUTH
Answering Our Kids' Questions Honestly

Holly and I heard somebody say we need to tell our kids the truth when it comes to their questions; otherwise they will no longer come to us with them. They will ask their friends or just Google it—especially if we as parents scold them for asking difficult or uncomfortable questions.

Knowing what to do is often easier than doing it. Such was certainly the case the night my daughter learned about the birds and bees and a few other life lessons.

Holly and I always thought three kids was the right number for our family. We both came from families of three kids, so it just felt right for us. Our third child, Kaleb, had just turned five months old, so we felt we were in the clear for me to go ahead and get a vasectomy.

I scheduled the vasectomy to happen in December, so it would qualify in that year's health insurance. Unfortunately, I received a call from the doctor's office saying the doctor decided to go on a vacation, so they were going to reschedule the appointment for a few weeks later, in January.

What?! Now my December appointment was being pushed into the next year, so our strategy of saving on medical benefits was lost. When I got home, I walked right into the kitchen and, not thinking about who was within earshot, I said, "Hon, I am so bummed because they rescheduled my surgery!"

Before I knew it, Kiley, our oldest who was seven at the time, came running into the kitchen, "Dad! Dad! What surgery do you have to have? Are you OK?" I didn't want Kiley to worry, and

Holly and I made eye contact in a way that I knew she agreed we should tell her.

"Well," I said, "Dad is having a surgery called a vasectomy, so Mom and I can't have any more kids. Mom and I are very blessed and grateful to have three kids, but we don't believe we are being called to have anymore."

Kiley replied, "Well, *Dad*, what do *you* have to do with making babies?"

I did not see that question coming, but I wanted to honor our honesty value. So I explained how the male body part goes inside the female, and then the male part releases sperm into the female body, which is how the baby is made. I told her the doctor will cut these things, like wires in my body, so the sperm does not release, thus Mom and I can no longer make babies. I got through that part and was feeling a sense of relief, thinking I was done, and the conversation was over.

Not so fast.

Kiley connected the dots on that idea to another question bouncing around in her head. "Well, then how will Cassidee and Ashley have a baby since they don't have a penis?" Cassidee, my sister, is a lesbian and is married to Ashley. We had discussed the lesbian topic in our house, but never about how they would have children.

Still wanting to continue the idea of always speaking truth, I said, "Well, you are correct, lesbians are not designed to have children naturally. So there are a few ways for homosexuals to have kids, one of which is adoption."

Now the questions were nonstop.

"What is adoption?" she said.

"Adoption is when a woman gets pregnant and doesn't want to keep the baby, so she puts it up for adoption. Then someone else can adopt the child."

I don't know if she was satisfied with that answer or not, but she was already moving on to the next question in her head.

"So is that what Abee's friend will do?" she asked. Say what? I thought. Abee is our niece, who was a freshman in high school at the time. What was going on with her?

This conversation was moving way too fast! I still had my sport coat hanging over my shoulder because I had just walked in the door. As I was trying to navigate this conversation, I looked over Kiley's head and saw in the background Holly pacing back and forth holding Kaleb on her chest, and she was biting her lip, doing the best she could not to laugh out loud.

"So what is going on with Abee?" I asked. Kiley shared that when she was with Abee recently, Abee saw on Facebook a friend of hers from high school was pregnant and planning to give the baby up for adoption.

"Yes, if Abee's friend gives her baby up for adoption, then couples like Cassidee and Ashley can adopt. Does that make sense?'

"Yes," Kiley said, "I think that is enough for now," she walked out.

Holly and I just stared at each other: *What just happened?!* What we thought was going to be a quick conversation about a vasectomy turned into a conversation covering the birds and bees, homosexuality, high school pregnancy, and adoption.

The very next morning I took the kids to school, and that day we were also taking the eighth-grade neighbor girl. As we are driving to school, I see our neighbor has a very thick book on her lap. I ask her what the book is, and she says it is about the Holocaust. Inquisitive Kiley asks, "What's the Holocaust?" and our neighbor gives a great, brief description of the Holocaust.

From the back of the minivan, Kiley looks in the rearview mirror, so she and I are making eye contact, and then says, "Well, Dad, I have learned a lot these last two days." I started tearing up right then and gave a quick laugh of relief, "Yes you have, babe."

Did Holly and I do that perfectly? No. Should we have waited or done it differently? Maybe. Yet we are so grateful we did it on the spot because not only have we had some great laughs since then about that conversation but also because Kiley knows we are a source of truth for her. She knows she can bring questions to us. I am blown away and humbled by the conversations we have and the issues and topics she shares with us.

There are numerous benefits to being a source of truth for your kids. You control the answer they get and how it is communicated, and you can respond to any follow-up questions they have. You also understand what they are processing and going through as kids or young adults. I also love that we can add parental wisdom if needed, as well as support it with biblical truth or have them think about it with a God filter.

I know other parents who have the same idea of always speaking truth. My cousin has what they call the "safe couch," where his boys can talk to them about anything and they are "safe" from getting in trouble.

DON'T TAKE YOURSELF SO SERIOUSLY
That Time I Asked for Sex Toys at McDonald's

I like to think of myself as a fairly competent person. I have a civil engineering degree and an MBA, and I have been blessed to hold some corporate executive positions. However, when I go through fast food drive-thru lines, my brain turns off. I never go through them by myself, so I don't get a lot of practice, but on family vacations we go through them a few times during a trip.

When I pull up to the speaker to order, something happens. All of the options to choose from, the pressure to decide whether I want to eat healthy or chubby, plus all the kids in the car yelling out what they want. I don't know if this makes me shut down the smart part of my brain, but something weird yet very funny happens.

One of these trips we went to McDonald's. We were in the drive-thru, and the kids were all telling me their orders, and Holly was helping organize and communicate the order to me. At this point I was not even thinking, I was just repeating into the drive-thru speaker what she was saying to me.

Our youngest at the time still ate Happy Meals. So my wife, being the great mother she is, wanted to make sure our son got the boy toy that McDonald's puts in the Happy Meal instead of him accidently getting the girl toy and being upset.

After I ordered the food, Holly said, "Make sure to get a boy toy." I have no idea why I didn't just repeat what she told me to say, but for some reason I improvised.

I asked the lady over the speaker. "Do you have sex toys?" She didn't answer, so I said it again, and a little louder and slower in case she didn't hear me. "Excuse me, ma'am, do you have sex toys?" No answer again, so I asked again louder, slower, and more frustrated.

Perplexed, I looked over at Holly to see what I am missing, and she was laughing so hard she was crying and couldn't talk. Right then it hit me! I was asking for sex toys, not gender-specific toys.

I was thinking sex as in gender of the kid, not naughty sex toys.

I quickly said, "Ma'am! Ma' am! Ma' am! I am so sorry. I am so sorry, I meant gender-specific toys, like for a boy or girl. I need a toy for a boy. Not sex toys!"

She was slow to respond because she too was laughing so hard she couldn't talk. It was awesome. We got it figured out, and when we pulled up to the window to actually get our food, and our sex toy, we had a great laugh with the McDonald's lady.

My family and I still laugh at that, plus other drive-thru stories. The humor in our house is alive because we laugh at our mistakes and move on. The intention in our parenting with our kids is to have fun, laugh a lot, and not take ourselves too seriously. We try to balance between play and purpose in the family.

This freedom of not taking ourselves seriously allows our kids to know they can take risks and make mistakes. They can try a new sport, a lemonade stand, a new DIY craft. Because our kids know they can "laugh it off," they have more openness to taking risks to advance their ideas and beliefs.

Our church in Cincinnati, Crossroads, uses the term "Aggressive Mistakes" to refer to bold risk-taking, and I love it. I want our kids to know we go after goals, dreams, and tasks aggressively, knowing there will be failures along the way. When those failures happen, we will tweak, modify, and realign our efforts. Mistakes are how we learn.

This attitude of not taking ourselves too seriously, along with how we praise boldness to try new things, creates a healthy environment where our kids grow.

RECALIBRATION QUESTIONS

1. As you read the honesty section, is there a question your child is asking that you are avoiding answering with the truth? Why?

2. When was the last time you had fun with your family? Laughter and excitement?

3. Do you have the posture of humility in your family where you can laugh at your mistakes and encourage your kids to do the same?

20

HOW WE DO LIFE TOGETHER

The Kind of Time We Want to Spend Together— Present and Intentional

So much of cultivating a healthy dynamic in our families comes down to something very simple—how we spend time together. Two common traps we all fall into for family time is not being present when in the same house, and not owning our calendars but letting them own us.

There are times when we are all in the same house and we need to do our own thing. We are tired and want some alone time. Somebody wants to read; maybe somebody else wants to watch a particular sports game. Other times there is something that needs to get done such as a work project or a kid's homework. Those alone times are understandable, and necessary. However, when that becomes the norm and not the exception, then isolation is created in the family even though everyone is in the same house at the same time.

Time must be created where the family spends time together. Playing board games, watching a movie and talking about it, going to activities together, eating meals as a family. Creating family unity takes discipline. Cell phones and tablets get in the way of us spending time together. We must put them away for blocks of time when at home.

On a road trip a few years ago, our family was impressed to see the creativity a Chick-fil-A operator had to stop technology from interrupting family meal time. Brad Williams is a Chick-fil-A operator in the Atlanta area, and he created the "Cell Phone Coop." If customers turn their phones to silent and put them in the cardboard cell phone coop, then after they eat, they all get a small ice cream cone for completing the challenge.

Brad Williams said in *Inside Chick-fil-A*, "My kids know when they sit down for a family dinner, they can't be using their cell phones or any other technology. This is the way I was raised—to truly value meaningful conversation around the dinner table." Knowing the importance of this value in his own family, he wanted other families to experience it as well.

It is sad that we have to be incentivized to talk to each other at the dinner table with a small ice cream cone, yet it is a reminder that we all battle with this. We need to make sure we are not only intentional about spending time with our family but also being mentally present when we do.

BE PRESENT—BOTH MENTALLY AND PHYSICALLY
"Don't Give Others the Best, and We Get the Rest"

I had the opportunity to interview some key business leaders as part of a leadership series for Venue magazine in Cincinnati. One common theme in the interviews was discussing the balance of home and work and how important it is. Yet we all relate to the all-too-familiar example many of us have experienced where we go to a work dinner with someone we may never see again and give our best by asking questions, caring, listening, and being funny, yet when we come home, we have nothing to give. We sit on the couch and watch a sports game. We open up our laptop and check emails. We don't ask our family how their day was. If we do ask, we may not even listen to their response.

We can be guilty of doing this right outside our own homes. We may be fighting inside with our spouse or kids, yet when we go outside to get the mail or take out the trash and run into a neighbor, it is game on. We are super happy and talkative. You would think it was the best day ever. Deep down we have the energy, but sometimes we only use it for strangers and neighbors.

We even see this in our kids at different times. I remember at one point we were having some tough weeks with our nine-year-old daughter, Kamdyn. She was very low energy in the house, in a bad mood, not very talkative, short tempered. My wife and I went to a parent-teacher conference prepared to hear the bad news, how our daughter was being a pain, not paying attention in class, bossing people around during group play, not sharing toys or ideas. We were at the edge of our seats waiting to hear the news.

We got the exact opposite report. The teacher said our daughter was one of her favorite students—always raised her hand in class, led group activities, helped other kids, and the list went on. We were so grateful and proud, but also perplexed and confused. To be honest, we were even a little mad.

How come the teacher and other students got the best of our daughter, yet we got the worst? The reality is, she does what we all do. She was giving the best to people at school, gymnastics, and other places outside the home, yet when she was home, she had nothing left to give.

We drew the line in the sand. We were no longer going to allow our daughter to operate that way. Nor could we. We could not continue to give the best of ourselves to the outside world and then treat our loved ones like crap. There had to be a better way.

The motto in our house is: "Don't give others the best, and we get the rest."

What does that look like? We each have to rally after a long day at school or work and be present with our family. At the dinner table we have conversations and talk about each other's day. No phones at the dinner table, and everyone is mentally present. Don't get me wrong. We have down time in our house; we're not always in interview mode. But we make sure we are caring about each other like we do for the business meal we have with someone we may never see again.

Just having this motto in our home is great because if any of us are having an off day, we can bring this phrase up and it helps us recalibrate. Vocabulary creates culture, and since we are all aware of this phrase, we can get on the same page quickly.

Does this mean you don't give your best at work so you can give your best at home? Not at all. You'll find that when you're giving your best at home, you have more in the tank to give at work! We are the ones who give ourselves permission to crash when we get home. We accept the idea that it is OK to crash on the couch. Sometimes we even think we deserve it because we worked so hard that day.

Our family deserves more. Our spouse had just as challenging a day as we did, some days worse. Our kids may have had a difficult day, or maybe they had an amazing day and they are just waiting for you to ask them about it. If we choose every day not to engage with our family when we get home, we create distance between us and them.

When you engage with your family members, they know they matter. You build confidence and security. They can dream bigger because they know you will be alongside them on the ride. If it is always about you, they will think they don't matter. They will begin to feel isolated and limited.

Begin the mindset shift now. On your way home from your next work dinner or long day, turn the radio off and start to pray, think, meditate, or whatever gets your heart realigned. During that drive home, give thanks for a great work dinner and maybe the new relationship or partnership that was established. From this position of thanks, ask for energy to engage with the family at a higher level. Ask for grace and patience as the kids may be extra loud or crying or the dog may be barking. More times than not, you will have a better mindset as you walk into your home, and you will be able to engage.

Give your family more because they deserve it and because it sets them up for greater success in life.

THROW DOWN SOME ANCHORS
From Floating through Life to Doing Life Together

A critical part of winning at home is being proactive and setting up rhythms the family can count on. Predictable patterns create a consistency with family members that foster a sense of security.

A lot of us float through life. Float through our career. Our marriage. Our parenting. We may be physically present, but mentally we are just hovering. Meeting to meeting during the work week and kid activity to kid activity on the weekend.

This may have come to light for you recently when people asked, "What was the best part of the last few months?" and you were left to say, "Uhh . . . nothing really stands out." Or you mention the vacation or the promotion. We either have nothing to say or we mention a one-time event.

If this is your situation now—the reality is, it happens to all of us at different times—I encourage you to stop floating and throw down some anchors! Those we lead at work or home need it. We need to be influencing and making a lasting impact for those we lead. Instead of just creating a highlight reel experience with a family vacation, create a predictable pattern that builds a foundation for character development.

At our house, every night of the week consists of dance, soccer, or gymnastics for our kids, I may have a work meeting, or my wife and/or I may have a social engagement. Not long ago we began this pattern of floating through the week as a family, waiting to catch up with each other on the weekend, *if* we weren't too tired from the busy week! I realized it was time for us to throw down an anchor. Since we did not have any kid activities on Wednesday nights, we chose that night to be family night.

We didn't want this to be just a pizza and movie family night, which are needed as well. We wanted to add some flair by empowering the kids, teaching life skills, and giving them ownership of the evening. We decided each one of us, including me, would take a turn cooking with my wife. Whether it is me, who gets stressed out in the kitchen, or our five-year-old son, who needs a stool to reach the counter, we went for it and have not looked back!

Predictable patterns not only create security, they give us something to look forward to as a family. When our family knows one of our predictable patterns like the Wednesday night dinner, move night, or our annual "staycation," they know the night is going to be fun because we will be together.

Another benefit of inviting our kids into our Wednesday night dinner is creating moments of leadership and empowerment. The evening before my five-year-old son, Kaleb, was to cook his selection of hamburgers, I asked the kids for any prayer requests. My son said he wanted to "be safe tomorrow and not get hurt." Shocked and curious about what was happening in his world, I asked, "What do you need to be safe at buddy?" He said, "Grilling!" What?! My son had taken the idea of helping cook hamburgers to the next level by expecting he would be the one grilling the hamburgers. I loved his eagerness and ownership, so I took him up on it and had him help flip the burgers that night. Seeing his chest puffed up with pride was well worth it.

One of the greatest wins from our predictable patterns is that our kids feel valued. They have heard Holly and me turn down invitations to make sure we are at home for family night. Our kids feel secure and know that they come before other people and activities on Wednesday nights. When your kids know they are loved and valued at home, this will help them navigate stresses and pressures outside the home.

Whether you choose a weeknight dinner, a weekend breakfast, or some other rhythm, pick something so you can put down an anchor in your family's life.

RECALIBRATION QUESTIONS

1. In the last week, were you managing your energy during the day so you had energy for your family when you got home?

2. What evening are you picking for a family dinner? Or if you can't do evening, what weekend day are you going to do a family breakfast or lunch?

21

YOUR FAMILY'S VISION

Where Is Your Family Headed?

About seven years ago I heard a guy from the Crossroads Church stage say something I've never forgotten: "Your family vision needs to be greater than the fifteen-year-old boys at school." In other words, if the family vision is not interesting, your teenage daughter's aspirations will go no further than the boys at school. This speaker's point was that the vision and purpose of your family has to be big enough to keep the family engaged and inspired.

When families do not have a purpose and are not going after something bigger than themselves, family members get bored. They look elsewhere for fun and adventure. They constantly play video games. They vape. They scroll social media endlessly. They drift. Now I am not saying the vision is to keep our kids from ever dating or getting married. Of course, we want that for them (if they want it for themselves), but at the right time and with the right partner.

By having a family vision and purpose, you elevate the expectations of what your children will want in a spouse and future family. Your children will not just settle for the funny class clown or the best athlete in the class or the prettiest girl or whatever is the draw. Instead, they will go after someone of character, which may still lead them to the best athlete, but that won't be the driving trait of the person. We want to encourage our kids to go after the heart of others, go after the inside and not the outside of the person, so we need to lead by example.

FAMILY VISION

Some of you may have never thought of the idea of writing a family vision statement. Up until a few years ago, I was in that same camp even though I spent time thinking about the company vision statement for the companies I worked for or the team I led at the time. In business, we all understand and expect to have a vision statement. Yet for the most important business that we lead, our family, we often neglect a vision statement. For some of us it is out of ignorance that we didn't know we should have one, while the rest of us thought about it but were intimated to get started. Maybe even a few of us wondered if it would even matter. As in business, teams that have a vision and remind each other of it are unified and going in the same direction.

Knowing that our families need a vision statement is the first step. Next, we need to create one. Drafting a family vision statement is hard because we want to make it perfect. My encouragement is, don't worry about it being perfect, just get it done. A perfect quote for this is: "Anything worth doing, is worthy doing messy." Once you get it done, you can start to modify it as you and your family grow into it.

When I work with clients, a verse on vision I like to reference is from the book of Habakkuk in the Bible. The prophet Habakkuk was complaining to God about God's silence and what Habakkuk believes to be inaction in regard to evil. In Habakkuk 2:2 God begins His response with, "Write the vision; make it plain on tablets, so he may run who reads it." A vision short enough that a runner can carry the correct message to others.

Similarly, our vision needs to be simple so that our family can understand it and explain it to others. And even if they don't tell others about it, it needs to be simple enough for them to remember it so they are more likely to live it out. When our children are in a difficult situation, they need to be able to remember the family vision so they can realign their hearts and make the right choice.

At Five Capitals we use a simple framework with clients to create their company and family vision and values. We call it the 5Vs: Vision, Values, Vehicles, Valuation, and Vocabulary. Please visit www.winathomefirstbook.com/resources to access a form that will help you develop your 5Vs.

Vision is what we feel we are called to do as a family. What is the good news that we are to share with others? Based on your family's experiences, giftings, and personalities, there is a unique way you can give to others.

Values has to do with who we are and how we act. We all have values as a family whether we call them out or not. Do you speak to your kids or yell at them? Do you spend time together and talk? Do you say one thing and do the other? Do you value work or sports over family? Is there a spiritual component to your family?

Vehicles are the ways we live out our vision and values as a family. These are activities you do frequently, on a predictable pattern, to help build your family and impact others.

Valuation relates to the ways we know we are winning in the world. Are we actually seeing movement with our family? Are we actually doing what we say our vision is?

Vocabulary are the words we do and don't say in our house. Words are powerful and create culture. We want to make sure we use positive instead of negative words. Encouraging and inspiring, instead of degrading or self-deprecating.

CARLSON 5VS

The following is my family's 5Vs. They are not perfect, nor do all of us have everything memorized, yet our family knows we have them.

- *Vision*: Rooted in God, we create a strong family unit to branch out to others to give love, hope, and laughter.

- *Values*: Who we are/how we act.
    Jesus—We love Jesus.
    Love—We love each other and others.
    Give—We give more than we receive.
    Together—We spend time together.
    Laugh—We have fun together.

- *Vehicles*: The ways we deliver our vision and values to the world.
    Spiritually—God at the center; attend church together and have family devotions/talks
    Relationally—family dinners; family adventures; date nights for Cory and Holly; dates with each kid; time with friends as family and individually
    Physically—vacations; sports/activities; family nights; attend kids' events together
    Intellectually—always learning

Financially—generous with our time, talent, and treasures through Crossroads Church, Five Capitals, Aruna, Changing Gears, The New Frontier, Kilgour School

- *Vocabulary*: The language we do and don't use.
    Do say:
    Please
    Thank you
    I love you
    You are forgiven
    I am sorry
    Great job
    Be bold
    Our yes means yes, our no means no
    Respect and protect
    Don't give others the best, and we get the rest

    Don't say:
    Sucks
    Hate
    I'm bored
    Cuss words
    Mean words to each other

- *Valuation*: How do we know we are winning?
    Couple—When we are truly connected and not just roommates.
        How many dates per month for Holly and Cory?
    Family—Happy, healthy kids who are showing love to each other and others.
        How many dates per month for each parent and kid?
    Community—When friends and neighbors see us as

a family working for the Kingdom in a loving, caring, genuine, nonjudgmental way.

How many guests over at our house per month?

RECALIBRATION QUESTIONS

1. What is the vision for your family?

2. What are your values?

Using the 5Vs form at www.winathomefirstbook.com/resources, work with your family to create your family's own 5Vs.

PART 4

WORK

"Whatever you do, work heartily, as for the Lord and not for men, knowing that from the Lord you will receive the inheritance as your reward. You are serving the Lord Christ."

Colossians 3:23–24

"In short, work—and lots of it—is an indispensable component in a meaningful human life. It is a supreme gift from God and one of the main things that gives our lives purpose. But it must play its proper role, subservient to God. It must regularly give way not just to work stoppage for bodily repair but also to joyful reception of the world and of ordinary life."

TIMOTHY KELLER
Every Good Endeavor: Connecting Your Work to God's Work

22

WHY AM I DOING THIS?

The Day I Realized My Vocational Purpose

A few years ago, I was involved in the rare experience of trying to sell a company from one ownership group to another. We
were owned by a small, boutique private equity company and
had grown to a size where it made sense to sell to a larger private
equity company to help fund and support our future growth. I
was president of sales for the company—one of four executives
responsible for presenting the company to the potential buyers.
My role was to help explain how we grew over the last few years
and cast vision for our future growth opportunities and plan.

During a six-week span we presented to eleven different private equity companies, and the schedule was the same for each.
The night the potential buyer arrived, we went out to a fancy

dinner and drinks. The next day we presented to them from 8 a.m. to 2 p.m. The process was intense but exciting.

Not only was it incredible to see how the private equity world works, providing significant growth in my business acumen, it was also a defining moment in my purpose. At one of these dinners the table conversation opened my eyes to what I had been wrestling with a lot. What was my purpose? What was I fighting for? Where was I headed? Why was I doing it? What was all this for? Did I want to stay in this career path? If we sold, would I go to another corporate role? Would I pack it all up and take the risk of starting over and pursue coaching since that is where my heart was and still is?

The table conversation became dominated by the topic of money. The guy who sat across from me was sharing with the table about his brand new $200,000 car. How fast it was, how it handled turns, and the sound of the engine. He even showed a YouTube video of the car, so we could see it and hear the purr of the engine.

I am not saying wealthy people are bad. I know amazing business people who are very wealthy, who also have been great mentors and friends of mine. The eye-opening part for me this particular night was to see the mindset of these individuals. When the topic went to family or home life, the conversation was shallow. I saw more passion for the sound of their car engine than for their kids or spouses.

That night I realized *what* I did no longer mattered. Instead, why I did my job was going to be my driver. Whether I worked at this company or another, my why was going to be about impacting others.

WHAT IS YOUR "WHY"?

About ten years ago Simon Sinek gave a talk that went viral. The video has over ten million views on YouTube and has been a common topic in the business world for the last decade. Simon talked about the difference between average and great companies. Average companies are about the *how* and the *what* of their operations, while great companies are about the *why* first, then the *how*, then the *what*.

Simon gave the example of Apple and how they start with why. Apple's *why* is "to challenge the status quo." Apple's *how* is to do this by making user-friendly products. Their *what* is they make computers, iPods, and many other products many of us use every day. Simon's overall idea is that people do not buy *what* you are selling, they buy the *why* behind it.

The *why* is the company's cause, belief, and/or purpose. Simon's talk was geared toward companies, but it applies to us as individuals as well.

When people tie their identity and life vision to *what* they do, they are setting themselves up for failure. When our identity is tied to the *what* of our work, it becomes the place we take our questions—our questions of value and worth. If we are doing great at work, we think we are amazing. If we perform poorly at work, we evaluate our own identity accordingly.

When work defines who we are, we can find ourselves putting work before family, our own health, and our personal well-being. We say no to family so we can work longer hours. We don't exercise so we can crank out a few more emails.

MY WHY

Shortly after that dinner, my *why* began to change. Instead of looking at my life through the lens of titles and what I did, I wanted my why to be helping leaders win at home and work. At the time I did not know I would eventually coach executives or even write a book, but my thought was to begin to impact those who reported to me. My *why* of helping people to win at home and work caused me to invest in my direct reports differently, equipping them with tools to succeed in both places.

Once I determined my *why*, it didn't matter what I did or where I worked. Yes, I still had a responsibility to execute well and grow the business, but my identity and purpose was no longer defined by the company purpose.

YOUR WHY

What is your *why* for your job? I like how, in his book *Every Good Endeavor: Connecting Your Work to God's Plan for the World*, Timothy Keller states: "A job is a vocation only if someone else calls you to do it for them rather than for yourself. And so, our work can be a calling only if it is reimagined as a mission of service to something beyond merely our own interests. Thinking of work mainly as a means of self-fulfillment and self-realization slowly crushes a person."

How can you reimagine your work so it is a mission of service to something beyond yourself, beyond just making money, beyond finding your identity in it? I have friends who are not passionate about the products their company makes (such as toilet paper), yet they have found their *why* to be about leading and developing the team they work with. On the other hand, I know people who are passionate about not only their team but also the good their service brings to other people, which in some cases literally can change their customers' lives (such as medical services).

RECALIBRATION QUESTIONS

1. What drives you at work? Your what or your why?

2. What is your why?

3. What decisions have you recently made that were driven by your identity being tied to work?

4. What decisions do you need to make differently so that you are making them based on your why being about something bigger than money or title?

23

BOUNDARIES *OUTSIDE* OUR WORK

A Framework for Balancing Work and the Rest of Life

I have many great memories from my childhood, but one in particular continues to stand out as my kids get older and my career develops.

My dad was at all my athletic events. I had two siblings, and we all played sports. They too remember him being at all of their games. I know he must have missed some, but we remember him at our games more than not being there.

I can still see him standing at the sidelines near the edge of the field I was on. For soccer he was near the goal we were trying to score on. For baseball he was on the first base side to watch me play second base.

My dad didn't have a cake job either. He always had a sales

management job that demanded he perform as well as travel. But to the best of his ability, my dad organized his travel to be home for our games and any other family events we had.

My dad's priority was his family.

We put our time wherever our value is.

Those who win at home have boundaries. The leaders I know who are winning at home have a set time they go home from work. They minimize the time they are on their computers at night and on the weekends. Great leaders have daily and weekly boundaries for their work and home life. Yes, occasionally they have to work late or on the weekends, but it is the exception for these leaders and not the norm.

FEAR AND CONTROL

Those who strive to win at work believe they can't miss any meeting, skip out on a work happy hour, or be slow to respond to an email, even during the weekend. When we get this mindset, we are being driven by two forces: fear and control.

We fear if we don't work hard enough then we will get fired, not get the next promotion, or not get enough new clients. When this fear kicks in, we then overswing believing we can control the situation. We tend to think if we're going to do well at work, we need to work all the time. We fall victim to the lie that we have 100 percent control over our business. We think we completely control our own destiny. But obviously this kind of thinking could not be further from the truth.

I see this play out in my life as I build my coaching practice when I think my business will not grow unless I am constantly sending emails to potential clients. Recently I was reminded how that is not the case when I had bronchitis for two weeks. I did not send any prospect emails because I was in bed sick, yet I landed two new clients from referrals during that time.

Don't get me wrong, we need to work hard while we are

working, but we don't need to work around the clock. A verse I remind myself and clients of is Psalm 127:1, *"Unless the Lord builds the house, those who build it labor in vain. Unless the Lord watches over the city, the watchman stays awake in vain."*

We have to believe that God has the night shift. If we are doing the right things during business hours, and the occasional overtime for projects or deadlines, then we must believe in God's provision for our life.

Conquering our fear of provision and performance will allow us to step away from work to engage in the other areas of our life.

WORK/REST

If we're going to do our best work, we will place our work within boundaries—boundaries that keep work from seeping into the rest of our life. We will make decisions about how much of our time work will get, and we will not let it have any more. That's a boundary between work and the rest of life.

The work/rest pendulum mentioned in part 1, "You," is a great filter to establish the rhythms and boundaries between work and the rest of our life. When we constantly are working or thinking about work, we never rest. Our constant striving at work will cause us to crash when we are away from work and with our family. We will end up working all the time, skipping our kids' activities. We will miss family meals because we are more concerned about letting down people at work than our own family.

When we are going to our work environment for our identity, we end up using the full tank of gas at work, and then the family just gets the fumes. Trying to constantly impress people at work with our effort or competency is mentally and physically draining. We overextend ourselves. Just like in trip planning, you need to manage your fuel to get to your final destination.

The key distinction in your energy management is to know where your destination is. We need to be honest with ourselves. Are you managing your energy to the end of the workday when you walk through the front door of home? Or are you managing your energy to the end of the entire day and your head hits the pillow at night?

It needs to be the pillow. Don't stop too early!

HOW TO GET BETTER

You need to manage your energy so you are not giving it all to work and still have capacity to be intentional with the family. Managing your energy means finding moments of solitude; exercising, praying, walking around the office building, eating right, going to bed on time, and napping are all ways to fill up the gas tank.

In addition, you need to look at ways to increase your gas efficiency as well. Being yourself rather than an imposter-self takes less energy. When I am my true self, it is life giving. I get energy from engaging with others. When I am insecure and in performance mode, it zaps me. Manage your fuel tank.

Leaders also set the stage for their families and their work teams. Instead of constantly driving for performance, encourage your team and family to find breaks.

Review the work/rest pendulum on a daily, weekly, monthly, quarterly, and annual process.

STAYCATION

A few years ago, our family was in the thick of it. I was busy traveling for work and our oldest was playing competitive soccer, so our weekends were busy with games and tournaments. Mixed in our schedule were social activities.

Even though we were trying our best to have our dates and family dinners, I knew our family needed a break and something to look forward to, like a mini-vacation. Unfortunately, we were in the middle of fall, so summer had passed, and Christmas was too far away.

We planned a *staycation*.

We made a hotel reservation for downtown Cincinnati, where we live. The plan was to eat downtown, swim in the hotel, and then wake up and spend the day walking around downtown. This staycation was what we needed as motivation to get through the busyness. We would get focused time with each other as well as the rest we all needed from the busy season, and it would refuel us for the months ahead.

Leading the family well means you also have to have monthly, quarterly, and annual moments for rest and reflection.

As a leader at work, you need to manage the team calendar the same way. If your team is busy, it's important to find ways to give them a break. Give them a day off, or a celebration dinner, or other ideas that encourage rest.

Without your leadership and nudge, individuals who value work over family never use all of their vacation time each year. They do not think work will survive without them, thus they never leave work.

As the leader goes, so goes the company. If you have boundaries, your team at work and home will take note. Having boundaries for when you are not working allows you to be focused and be present in the other areas of your life.

RECALIBRATION QUESTIONS

1. How can you make sure you and your team use all of your vacation days this year?
2. What meetings, happy hours, or associations do you need to say no to this month so you can be with your family?
3. If fear and control are hard for you this season, through pray and journaling ask God how to release those in your life.

24

BOUNDARIES *INSIDE* OUR WORK

A Framework for Becoming Strategic and Productive

A few years ago, I had been managing two different business lines for a few months and was running around like a chicken with its head cut off. The business lines rolled up to $50 million in revenue, so there was always something to be done, yet neither were performing well.

To make matters worse, they were both in the spotlight of our company's executive team. One of the business lines had new competition in the market that was more cost effective, thus our solutions were losing market share quickly. At the same time the other product line was now experiencing single-digit margins, opposed to double-digit margins in previous years, probably due to poor internal pricing strategy and structure.

During the early days of my leadership, I was only task oriented. I thought the harder I worked in the business, the better it would do. Putting out fires left and right, constantly checking email for updates or pushing out emails to the team. Deep down, I knew I should be strategic and work on the business, but I didn't think I had time for that. If I stopped to be strategic, then who would put out all the fires? Who would do the work?

Yet chasing fires across the country was not moving the needle on these two business lines. No matter how much I worked or hustled I needed a new strategy. A new plan.

At the time I was reading *The Accidental Creative* by Todd Henry, and he suggests a strategy I needed to try. Todd's idea of the "Big 3" is to devote time to the Big 3 areas in your life where you need a jolt of creativity. By identifying the Big 3, you are more likely at random times to get inspired with an idea for one of the three, whether from something you read, a conversation you have, or your own creativity.

A few pages later, Todd discusses the need to cluster our time to be more efficient and effective. Otherwise we are constantly multitasking between activities, thus never getting to any creative breakthrough.

I went for it and combined the two ideas and created the "Big 3 Strategy Session" for my two business lines. Adapting some of Todd's thoughts, plus my own spin, I created these sessions where I turned off my phone, did not look at email or any other distractions, and just focused on the Big 3. I used a whiteboard, post-it notes, computer (I stayed off email and other distractions), and whatever else would help me get creative.

During my career, I had strategy sessions before the start of a new fiscal year or a new initiative, but I had never tried recurring strategy sessions. I blocked out my calendar from 2 to 3 p.m. every Thursday, and this was a time I dedicated myself to being strategic. I did this every week for the rest of my time in that role.

I started the process and not only loved it, but it worked! I developed new ideas and implementation plans. Not all the ideas I came up were necessarily mine—they may have been something I heard—but I was able to hit pause and actually consider them.

Focusing on the Big 3 items allowed me to identify a few key partnerships to pursue, a pricing model for both businesses, as well as training and development programs for both lines. These ideas turned the business lines around to the point that the bottom line, also known as EBITDA (earnings before interest tax depreciation and amortization), quadrupled for one business and doubled for the other.

This would not have happened unless I lifted my head up from being in the business, took a break from the emails, and got creative, strategic, and more productive.

We need to set boundaries at work based on decisions about how often we will take time to work on our business versus working in our business. Thus, being intentional about how often we check email as well as hit pause on the tactical work to be strategic.

I AM TOO BUSY

When I propose this strategy to other business leaders in need of a creative jolt, the push back I often get is that they are too busy. They don't have time to take their eye off the day-to-day obligations.

My first response is often to share a humorous perspective of an old cartoon that illustrates this scenario perfectly. A man is struggling to push a wheel barrow because the tire is flat. In the cartoon, another man is offering him a new tire that is full of air. Yet the man pushing the wheelbarrow says, "No thanks. I am too busy."

That's so true! So often we are busy pushing something forward that is not working well, yet we won't stop to incorporate a better plan for fear of short-term loss.

After a few laughs at the cartoon, we then discuss common objections that you may be considering as well.

What about other company meetings that may take place?

Almost everybody in today's work environment has access to their colleagues' calendars to see if they are busy or free. I encourage clients, as I do myself, to put a meeting on their calendar called "Strategy," or whatever word is appropriate at their company. So as people were planning a meeting, if they saw I was busy from 2 to 3 p.m. on Thursday, they would schedule the meeting another time. Occasionally, the meeting organizer would contact me to see if I could move my other meeting because this time slot worked for many. I always told them, "Probably, let me look into it and see what I can do." Ha! I was the only one in the Big 3 meeting; of course it would work. However, the big item to note is I did not cancel my strategy session with myself. Instead I moved the time block to another opening in my calendar, ensuring I got to it at some point that week.

What about all the work that needs to get done?

Sounds odd, but a lot of it got done or progress was made. Matter of fact, during the Big 3 hour strategy session I had, some of the email exchanges that took place actually got solved by others while I was in my strategy session! If I had not been in that strategy session, I would have been participating in that exact same email exchange, thus not getting anything new done. The reality is that the decision the group arrived at with me not on the email exchange probably would have been the same had I been involved. For matters that were not solved and needed my attention, I could quickly hop in and solve them or provide next steps for the team.

EXPAND OR CONTRACT

In his book *Fanatical Prospecting*, Jeb Blount talks about how we will expand or contract our work based on the time allowed. We all have seen this play out in our own lives.

Parkinson's law says that work expands to fill the time allotted for it. We are all guilty of letting our work expand to fill too much of our time. We are tired or unmotivated and we let an easy two-hour task take all afternoon. We get distracted and look at social media, constantly check emails, and have random conversations at the water cooler. When we come to and decide it is time to start working again, most of us decide we better go to the bathroom and get some more coffee before we dive back into work. Yes, we may be at work, but we are not working very effectively or efficiently.

On the other hand, Mark Horstman's corollary to Parkinson's law is that we contract our work to the reduced time allowed. We see this during the week leading up to a vacation. It is amazing how much work we get done right before we are going to be out of the office for a few days. The phone call we dreaded to make, we make. We finish the document so somebody can review it while we are gone. We send emails before vacation so, hopefully, we get responses on our return. We can crank out some serious work right before a vacation!

WE NEED BREAKS TO BE CREATIVE

When we don't take breaks from work, we end up filling the time with busywork thinking that work won't survive without us. However, when we take breaks—like when we are on a plane, vacation, doctor's appointment, or even strategy sessions—we end up seeing that it continues on without us.

How does this affect you? No matter what our job is, we need to get strategic and creative from time to time. If our head is always down in the business, then we do not have the ability to think outside the box.

- A teacher needs planning sessions that are actually planning and not just task oriented.

- A salesperson needs strategy sessions to think about how to bring value to customers and not just sending out proposals and replying to emails.

- A CEO needs to think strategically on how to lead the culture for the company and key partnerships to open up new opportunities, not always be in the day-to-day business.

FOCUSED SESSIONS WORK

I have done variations of this over the years due to its effectiveness. For example, in writing this book, I could not gain any traction just trying to fit it into a normal workday. Also, the idea of writing "when I got inspired" didn't work either because I was always in task mode and not allowing for creativity.

Finally, I took action and set a few time blocks throughout the week when I would write, and during this time, I did not check emails or texts or do anything outside of writing. It was amazing when I was focused how much I got done. I also wasn't worried about what emails came in as I worked because I knew I would get to them when I was done writing.

It is important to step back and get an overall view of the business rather than what happens moment by moment. When our identity is tied to our business, we do not think we can stop to be strategic. Boundaries set inside our work not only allow us to stop being tactical for a strategic session but also enable us to realize we can detach from work all together for life outside of work.

RECALIBRATION QUESTIONS

1. How can you create blocks of time in your calendar to work on strategy for your business?

2. What task do you need to focus on?

3. What are your Big 3?

25

HOW DO YOU EMPOWER EMPLOYEES?

Be the Leader Who Elevates Employees

One of my favorite bosses was Max. He knew my wife's and my kids' names. He enjoyed it when we went out for dinner with our spouses. He knew it grew our friendship and also demonstrated gratitude for the sacrifice our spouses were making. He occasionally organized the sales team to go bowling and grab some beers. Max was very good about cultivating a relationship with his team.

Max also had high expectations. We worked hard to hit our sales numbers and provide accurate forecasting for the upcoming months. When we had a big presentation, he wanted us to practice together beforehand. He reviewed our expense reports. He read our emails and provided comments.

I didn't want to let him down as a friend but also as a leader. Max demanded excellence for himself and his team. He worked hard to create a top performing team.

NOT MAX

I have experience with another type of boss too. This other boss I worked for did not know my wife's name or how many kids I had, let alone their names. He never asked about my family or anything in my personal life. Instead, he always drove for more results.

When my phone would ring with a call from him, I knew it was not going to be an empowering call. On the Invitation vs. Challenge matrix (discussed in chapter 18), he was all Challenge. He regularly pointed out my mistakes and what I could have done better. My wife could always tell if had I talked with my boss that day because I was defensive, tense, and frustrated. Yes, I performed well for this boss when I was on the clock, but off the clock I was not committed.

AGAIN, NOT MAX

I also have had experience with another extreme. The buddy. The manager who created a cozy environment. This boss knew my wife's and my kids' names and activities. Every Friday he would ask what we were going to do on the weekend, and then every Monday he asked in depth about our activities. There is absolutely nothing wrong with being involved in your employee's personal life, but when boss/employee conversations are dominated by personal topics, you have to question if work is getting done.

This boss always forgave a missed deadline or an inaccurate forecasted sales number. His usual response was, "Don't worry, we will get them next time." Well, most often "next time" got the same nonconsequential response. As you can imagine, neither my team nor I lived up to our potential under this leadership style.

RELATIONSHIP AND RESPONSIBILITY

Maybe you can relate to the above three kinds of bosses too. Max's style of empowerment brought loyalty and commitment, whereas judgement and dictatorship brought self-destruction to everyone involved, and the cozy environment brought friendship, but it didn't yield results.

In chapter 18 of part 3, "Parenting," we introduced the Invitation vs. Challenge matrix. The lens to view this matrix at work is Relationship vs. Responsibility. Inviting employees into Relationship by asking about their home life, grabbing a beer with them, having fun. Challenging an employee into Responsibility to make sure the job gets done by holding people accountable, expecting a certain level of excellence due to the task.

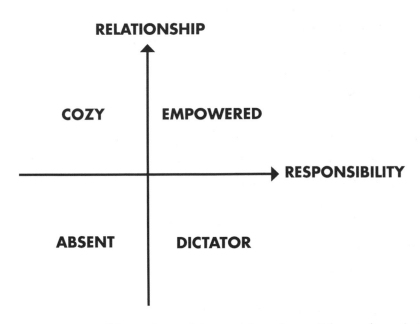

In my own life and working with others, I have found this tool to be incredibly valuable for situational leadership. There are times we need to calibrate and spend relational time with certain employees because we challenged them for a season, they succeeded, and now it's time to recalibrate. On the other hand, there may be other employees we have been soft on, so it's time to increase the intensity so they can grow.

A healthy leader understands how to use this concept based on the situation of the employee. However, unhealthy leaders don't understand, thus they stay in the same quadrant for all employees and at all times. They have a one-size-fits-all mentality. When this happens, it is most often due to the leader getting his or her identity from work. Where the leader ends up on the matrix is related to how the leader obtaining a sense of his or her own value.

Max did not go to work to get his identity. He had a strong family, he had hobbies, and he was secure in his identity. If he left the company, it would not devastate him. Max wanted both Relationship and Responsibility because he knew the combination would yield the best results for the team.

The second boss I mentioned did not want Relationship. Only results. He found his identity in not only work but the work performance. Leaders like this are driven by Responsibility and results instead of Relationship. Their drive for work could be a general ambition to perform well, or a desire to have their name on the leaderboard, or a drive to make a lot of money. These leaders do not ask questions about you personally; instead, they only want to make sure you submit your projects on time and correctly. They are not concerned with anything else. Frankly, these leaders view Relationship as a waste of time. Employees may march to the orders of this leader, but only when they're on the clock. Off the clock these employees are thinking about updating their resume, wondering where they will work next, as well as wishing the boss would move on.

The third boss I mentioned was about Relationship to a fault. Leaders who create a cozy environment often do this because they also are going to work for their identity, but for approval more than ambition. They want to be liked by everyone. Perhaps due to struggles at home and tension in their personal life, they want friends in their work life. They do not press in when people are not meeting their numbers. They do not hold people accountable for fear they will not be liked. Instead of having a tough conversation with employees who are not performing well, they give them a pass. Instead of balancing truth and grace, they are only grace.

The best leaders are those who empower. They drive both Relationship and Responsibility. They care about you and your career, but they also equip and empower you to be successful. These leaders are in the top right quadrant because they are constantly calibrating between Relationship and Responsibility.

HOW DOES THIS AFFECT HOME?

Leaders who understand their identity and lead others for empowerment are most often winning at home. They win at home because they are present with their family when at home. Empowering leaders have equipped their team, allowing them to delegate, which not only frees up time from tactical efforts but also gives them mental freedom to step away from work. Thus, when they are home, they are present. Even greater, they have the mindset that work can survive without them.

On the other hand, leaders who tie their identity to their work are often not concerned about home. They allow work to consume their time and mind twenty-four hours a day. Leaders who tie their identity to work performance are constantly thinking about how to win more clients, get more projects, do this and do that. Firing off emails to employees at all hours of the day and during the weekend. When they are with their family, they are not mentally present.

Cozy leaders at work usually fall into one of two camps. One

camp is those who are not winning at home due to lack of relationship or engagement, so they come to work to find their
friends and community. This leads to more time away from home
because they have another work happy hour to attend. Or when
they are at home, they would rather be with their work friends.
The other camp is the cozy leaders at work who are also cozy
at home. The reason this does not look like wining at home is
because they are getting walked over. The kids are dominating
the decisions, and the lack of backbone the parent has at home
carries over into the workplace.

RECALIBRATION QUESTIONS

1. Plot the people you lead in the Relationship vs. Responsi-
    bility matrix. Is it time to recalibrate?

2. If you currently have employees in cozy or dictatorship
    relationships, ask yourself why.

3. How can you bring more "Relationship and Invitation"
    into some of your work and even home relationships?

4. How can you bring more "Responsibility and Challenge"
    into some of your work and even home relationships?

26

HOW DO WE VIEW OUR COWORKERS?

Be the Leader Who Gives More than Takes

When we are at work and have things to get done, it's really easy to begin to see coworkers as obstacles rather than as people who are vital to the mission of the company.

A book I really enjoyed in recent years that further opened my eyes to this situation is *Leadership and Self-Deception*, by the Arbinger Institute. The main concept of this book is "in or out of the box thinking." "In the box thinking" is the idea that we surround ourselves with a belief, the box, and then are constantly motivated to justify staying in the box. Thus, self-deception of our surroundings.

The book states, "*Whether at work or at home, self-deception obscures the truth about ourselves, corrupts our view of others and our circumstances and inhibits our ability to make wise and helpful decisions."*

If we think an employee is a threat to our job or a barrier to our success, then anytime we see an action that verifies it, we feel justified to remain in the box. For example, if we feel a coworker is a jerk, then he can say five things, but if one of them is "jerky," we tell ourselves, "Yes, he's a jerk." We spend energy trying to justify our position. When we see others as a threat or competition, we may not share vital project details with them for fear it may push them ahead.

Whereas "out of the box" is thinking what is best for all involved. We are out of the box when we view people as people, not as objects or barriers. We see these people with their own hopes and dreams, their own brokenness and imperfections, just as we have our own. We have more humility rather than pride. More outward focus than inward. We are more about the team than ourselves.

"PEOPLE ARE IDIOTS"

Peter is a successful marketing executive with a Fortune 50 company I have been blessed to coach for the last eighteen months. One of the early stages in our coaching engagements is to have clients identify items in their personal and professional life that can be categorized in a few different categories: breakthrough, frustration, failure, and battle.

I was shocked to see what Peter had in the "frustration" category: *"people are idiots."* No joke! As we unpacked this more, Peter expressed that he did not have patience for people who were not as smart as him. He was extremely intelligent and had made it this far on competency and self-drive alone.

My role as a coach is to work with clients to grow in both competency and character. When competency outgrows character, bad things are bound to happen as pride gets in the way. This can lead one to become self-dependent and self-serving. On the other hand, if there is not growth in competency, then they can stagnate, become complacent, and ultimately be passed by the competition.

Investing in character development allows you to become self-aware, humble, and God-dependent. This puts you in a posture to serve others as you continue to grow in competency, leadership, and opportunity.

A great book, *Lead Yourself First*, by Raymond M. Kethledge and Michael S. Erwin, shows the difference between good and great leaders to be the discipline of solitude. Through interesting stories, they provide evidence of how solitude brings leaders clarity, creativity, emotional balance, and moral courage. A true and convicting quote in the book is from James Mattis, a retired four-star Marine Corps General: "An effective leader is the person who can maintain their balance and reflect, when a lot of people around them are reacting. If I was to sum up the single biggest problem of senior leadership in the information age, it's a lack of reflection."

So as the weeks progressed, Peter and I worked on practicing solitude, self-reflection, journaling (which he had never done before), and treating people as people, not a threat or a means to an end. On our eighth call a light bulb went on for him.

"I have a really weird story to tell you," he said.

"Awesome, tell me."

"No, this is really weird. I feel like an idiot saying it."

"I hear all kinds of things on these calls; nothing is weird at this point."

"Well," Peter went on, "the other day, I was in a boardroom meeting and, I know this is going to sound weird, but I felt that I could hit pause on the meeting, zoom out, and watch myself and others in the meeting."

I was ecstatic. We were getting transformation! "That is

amazing!" I said. "Well done! You are starting to see people as people. You are growing in emotional intelligence. You are growing more secure in your identity. You used to have to win every argument or make sure you said the smartest thing in the room. Instead, you are now thinking, 'I don't need to have the last word.' Or, 'I don't need to win this argument or point; instead, Suzy can have it.' You are seeing the bigger picture instead of your small world."

Our story is a part of a much greater story. Until we choose to participate in the greater story, we will always be fighting small, irrelevant battles.

We all struggle with wanting to care just for ourselves because we have been told, "If you don't watch out for yourself, no one else will." Yes, there may be some instances of that, but the majority of the time, evidence shows it is better to give than to take.

LEADERS ARE GIVERS

Give and Take is a great book by Adam Grant in which he unpacks his study of thousands of individuals in different fields. The book found that in all industries, "takers" start off fast in their careers but then start to plateau. "Givers," on the other hand, may have a slower start, but then they have rapid growth later when the relationships they built and people they served start to give back.

Takers, as Grant explains, generally take from others more than they give. They take recommendations, referrals, contact information, advice, contributions, etc., more than they offer any of those items to others. Generally speaking, they like to get more than they give. Takers see the world as a competitive, dog-eat-dog world. So they do a lot of self-promotion and making sure they get the credit for their efforts. Takers are not necessarily evil, they just have the mindset that if they don't look out for themselves, no one will.

On the other hand, givers are others-focused. They serve, they help, they are open to providing input that will benefit others. Grant does point out in the book, when givers are not careful, they can be stepped all over. Givers who have boundaries in place make everyone around them better. The idea that a rising tide raises all boats.

Takers' identity is most often tied to their success or performance at work. They are willing to burn bridges if it makes them look good.

When our identity is tied to our success at work, then other people become obstacles, barriers, threats to our success. However, when our identity is not found in work, others are viewed as important people who can help the company achieve its goals. These individuals are givers. They see a greater picture.

Since that breakthrough call, Peter has continued to grow in his ability to see others as people instead of threats or obstacles to his goals. He sees them as vital to getting the job done.

RECALIBRATION QUESTIONS

1. Are you viewing your coworkers as competition or collaborators?

2. Are you giving more than you are taking?

3. What is a frustration you currently have in your job? What is one step you can take to move toward a breakthrough?

27

IT'S NOT JUST ABOUT THE SALE

How to Build Trust with Your Customers

We all need to think of work as a "get to," not a "have to." You are blessed to have your job, and although there may be other things you wish you were doing, I am sure you can also list a ton you are glad you are not doing!

Starting from a place of gratitude can have a big impact on how we view and interact with our customers.

When work is a "have to," then we are just focused on the end result and not the journey. We know we have to work, so we just do the bare minimum to make sure we get to the end on time and without much pain. Our thought is if we invest too much in one relationship or another, then there will not be time to do the work. With this lens, we often see our customers as a means to an end. We don't want to invest in them for fear it will take too much time and energy.

However, when we start to view work and interactions with clients as a "get to" instead of a "have to," new possibilities develop.

STEER WRESTLING

The majority of my sales career was in the construction industry selling to contractors. Those who know me can attest I am the complete opposite of a contractor. I prefer hair gel over hats, stripe dress socks instead of thick white socks, and trendy jeans over Wrangler pants.

It was only because I cared personally and professionally for my customers that they bought from me; I was not "their kind." Actually, some of my best customers were the ones who were the most different from me!

When we moved to Colorado, we had a distributor who did some work with us, purchasing corrugated metal pipe from our company and selling it locally. As region manager, I saw more potential and knew this was an opportunity to get a business win. But in the process, I got much more.

As I spent time with Buddy and Paula, owners of this distributorship in Colorado, and took an interest in them, we started to build a relationship on genuine connection. In addition to our common business interests, I was intrigued by their personal interests as well. Buddy and Paula lived on acreage and owned animals, and their mission was to make an impact on youth in their area.

Buddy had been a great steer wrestler, so they invited young men over to their house and taught them how to steer wrestle. Along the way they also taught them life lessons and invested in them personally.

As our relationship continued to grow, they invited me to

their house to try steer wrestling. It was amazing! Buddy taught me how to steer wrestle over a couple of visits. One of the visits my family came along, and we stayed a few nights at their house. My wife and I even traveled to Las Vegas with Buddy and Paula to watch the National Finals Rodeo show where I bought my one and only pair of cowboy boots!

Friendship and incredible memories were the greater prize, but truth be told, as the relationship grew, so did the results. This distributor became one of the largest in the country for our company.

Not every customer will become your best friend, but we all can improve our relationships with our customers by caring more about them and less about ourselves—more about the relationship than the results.

MAKING THE SHIFT

Shifting into relationship mode can be difficult for a lot of us because of our own insecurities and agendas. Traveling salespeople all have the same thoughts running through our heads when we walk into a client's office: Where is the family picture so I can ask questions about their kids? Where is the college logo so I can talk about college football? Where is the interesting piece of art or vacation picture that I can ask about?

If this is you, you're not alone. We all are thinking the same thing.

Let's keep going with the salesperson example and see what happens. I realize not everyone reading this is a traveling salesperson, but hopefully this example will help you imagine how to make this shift in your own context.

So how do you set yourself apart and truly connect? It starts with having the intention of building relationship and trust instead of just making small talk with hopes of getting the sale. We build for relationship and not for transaction.

I see no better model than how Jesus interacted with others. Jesus cared for the women at the well (John 4:1–45). Even though it was not politically correct to talk to a woman then and there, He took the time and the risk to ask her questions. He asked questions about her marriage, and He already knew the answer!

We can begin to better understand our clients by asking questions. Go deep by asking questions like: Why do you work here? What do you do for fun? How do you balance work and family?

The next step is to actually care about what they say. I know this sounds trite, but the client can feel whether or not you care. Do you ask the same surface-level questions as every other sales person? Or do you take it a step deeper?

For example, perhaps your client shares that his daughter is starting college. Most salespeople end the conversation there with, "That's great your daughter is a freshman in college this year."

If you are showing you actually care, your next question could be, "How are you and your spouse handling the new transition?" Now you are building relationship!

While you're at it, try to discover their reason for buying your product or service. We cannot assume their reasons for buying are the same as the customer down the street. Maybe they want a permanent solution. Maybe they want a temporary solution.

I find it so interesting that Jesus always asked the sick if they wanted healing, even if He could tell they were paralyzed or blind!

Seek to get to know their pain points. Don't assume you know what they need. In Jesus's interactions, some sick people wanted to be healed, while others wanted their sins forgiven. Understand your clients' needs so you can later position your product as the right solution.

BRING JOY

Generally, customers have plenty of options when it comes to people they can buy from. They want to connect to places and people who are positive. Staying positive and joyful can be challenging when it's been a long week. But your clients don't need your negative energy or frustration brought into their office.

God has you here at this moment. Lean into it! When you bring positivity into your job, joy will pour out of you and connections will be cultivated.

You've probably heard the saying, "People don't buy from people they know, but from people they trust." Customers truly do want to buy from people they like and trust and who show they care.

Take some time to dig into each of these areas. See where your strengths lie and where you can improve!

RECALIBRATION QUESTIONS

1. How can you view your job as a "get to" rather than a "have to"?

2. What are some ways you can invest in some of your customers' conversations so they build relationship and are not just about the transaction?

NEXT STEPS

THANK YOU FOR READING THIS BOOK.

My prayer is that implementing these tools and concepts will help you, your family, and your team thrive.

I know you'll face challenges and setbacks. We all do. Oftentimes, clients will get on a coaching call with me and start venting. At some point they say they can't believe how much they have been complaining about their personal and professional life. When I tell them almost all calls go this way and that they are not alone, they are so relieved to hear it.

Here's the key to success in life: how quickly you recalibrate.

We do this visual in Montana at The New Frontier. Imagine you have a compass that you align to True North, and you set an endpoint on that path a few hundred feet away.

Now imagine that instead of walking directly to the endpoint, you walk at a one-degree difference. With each step, you are getting farther away from the endpoint. Yes, you may be walking in the direction of the endpoint, but if you keep at that bearing one degree off of True North, you will end up away from the endpoint. But if you would have recalibrated along the way, you could have hit the target!

Leaders don't always get it right, but they have the humility to recalibrate and get back on the right track.

KEEP RECALIBRATING!

ACKNOWLEDGMENTS

This is the first book I have written, so I have a lot of people to thank.

First and foremost, I thank God for the story of restoration in my life. For not only meeting me in my valleys, but not letting me stay there. Instead, equipping and empowering me to share my story with others. I pray the success of this book, speaking engagements, and whatever else may be a result of my story, is for Your glory and not mine.

Holly—Wow. As I relived the stories writing this book, I was once again blown away by your grace, mercy, forgiveness, and love. You model Jesus in so many ways. Thank you for being my wife, mother of three amazing kids, and my best friend.

Kiley, Kamdyn, and Kaleb—thank you for being incredible kids and making it easier to win at home. I pray this book is a guide that will help you live life to the fullest and you each become an amazing light for the Kingdom.

My parents—thank you for showing us how to live with incredible faith, a healthy marriage, positive parenting, and a strong work ethic.

Casey, Cassidee, and your families—thanks for the love and laughs over the years. We have been through a lot as siblings, yet had a blast, so thank you.

Ron, Veda, Nicole and Jay—thank you for never giving up on me even though I wasn't always the best son-in-law or brother-in-law. Thank you for your love and support.

Brandon and Sarah Davison-Tracy—you guys help dreams come alive, even when I didn't know it was a dream! You encourage and inspire people to find something they didn't know they had inside. Whether it was painting on canvas, writing a book, or numerous other dreams—thank you.

Aunt Suzie—your constant encouragement, support, and unconditional love has always been a model for me as a way to live out my faith. Thank you.

Brandon Schaefer—thank you for your support and wisdom the last six years. Your content and coaching are a huge contributor to the man I am today—leader, coach, father, and husband.

Chad Allen—thank you for the patience and accomplishment of taking a 50,000-word mess from a civil engineer and not a writer and turning it into a book that actually flows and is helpful to readers. You knew my heart to get this message to others, so I appreciate the extra time spent on the project.

Chris Hartenstein—your wisdom and generosity are unbelievable. Thank you for being the bridge from corporate America to full-time coaching. You also helped me better understand living my identity as a son, which has forever changed my life, as well as my wife and kids. Thank you.

Past and present clients—thank you for being on the journey with me. Without your humility to be coached, I would not have been able to make the transition from executive leader to executive coach. Thank you for your vulnerability, as well as friendship along the way.

Crossroads Church – Brian Tome, Chuck Mingo, and others that create content and inspiration. Kim Botto for submitting my name for the leadership program that fueled my career change. The Crossroads community that has provided friends, small groups, and great experiences.

Friends who endorsed *Win at Home First*—I know endorsing a book is not an easy task as you must read the book, provide the endorsement, plus take the risk of associating your name to a book and author. Thank you for taking the time and risk.

Friends who read versions of my book before it was complete—thank you. Being my first book, I didn't realize how many iterations there would be. I apologize, and thanks for being there every step of the journey.

New friends that helped me write, edit, and lay the book out— thank you. Lois Stück, My Word! Publishing, Jen Kolic, Andrea Constantine, Victoria Wolf, and Polly Letofsky.

If you are not on the above list but involved in my life—thank you. Your smile, your timely words of encouragement, your support reading my emails, and many more actions are all needed, and I couldn't do it without you. Thank you.

Bring **WIN AT HOME FIRST**
and these proven success principles to your family,
team, and organization.

To work with Cory, or invite him to speak at your next event, contact him at cory@corymcarlson.com.

Learn more at corymcarlson.com as well as sign up for Cory's weekly email he sends out to clients and friends.

ABOUT THE AUTHOR

Cory M. Carlson has helped leaders around the world develop happier and more fulfilling lives. Now, he's sharing his expertise in a new book, *Win at Home First*.

As an entrepreneur, former executive, husband, and father of three, Cory M. Carlson understands the pressures working parents face. He is passionate about helping business leaders win both at work and home.

Twenty years in corporate America gave Cory amazing opportunities, as he worked his way up to the executive level. But he also saw brokenness: work without purpose, strained marriages, and absentee parents. Business leaders especially were often not living life to the fullest. When Cory discovered coaching, it helped him become a better leader, husband, and father. So, he left his corporate career to help other leaders achieve a healthier work-life balance.

Cory holds an MBA from Rockhurst University, and a Civil Engineering degree from the University of Missouri. Currently, Cory lives in Cincinnati with his awesome wife and three amazing children.

Cory is an author, speaker, and executive coach. To hire him to speak at your event and teach your group how to balance the responsibilities of home and work, please connect with him on social media @carlsoncory or at www.corymcarlson.com.

Made in the USA
Columbia, SC
09 November 2022

70706651R00133